D0283017

The Only Clutter Control Book You'll Ever Need

Fast, Easy Ways to Clean Up the Mess and Conquer the Chaos

Edited by
Andrea Mattei

with contributions from
Bob Adams, Eve Adamson,
Katina Z. Jones, and Jason Rich

Adams Media
Avon, Massachusetts

Copyright © 2004, F+W Publications, Inc. All rights reserved.
This book, or parts thereof, may not be reproduced
in any form without permission from the publisher;
exceptions are made for brief excerpts used in published reviews.

Published by Adams Media,
an F+W Publications Company
57 Littlefield Street
Avon, MA 02322
www.adamsmedia.com

ISBN: 1-59337-022-9

Printed in Canada.

J I H G F E D C B A

Library of Congress Cataloging-in-Publication Data
Mattei, Andrea.
The only clutter control book you'll ever need / Edited by Andrea Mattei.
p.   cm.
ISBN 1-59337-022-9
1. House cleaning. I. Title.
TX324.M374 2004
648'.5—dc22
2003028005

Contains material adapted and abridged from *The Everything® Time Management Book* by
Bob Adams, ©2001, Adams Media Corporation; *The Everything® Stress Management Book*
by Eve Adamson, ©2002, Adams Media Corporation; *The Everything® Feng Shui Book*, by
Katina Z. Jones, ©2002, Adams Media Corporation; and *The Everything® Organize Your
Home Book* by Jason Rich, ©2002, Adams Media Corporation.

This publication is designed to provide accurate and authoritative information with
regard to the subject matter covered. It is sold with the understanding that the publisher is not engaged in rendering legal, accounting, or other professional advice. If legal
advice or other expert assistance is required, the services of a competent professional
person should be sought.
    —From a *Declaration of Principles* jointly adopted by a Committee of the American
        Bar Association and a Committee of Publishers and Associations

Many of the designations used by manufacturers and sellers to distinguish their products are claimed as trademarks. Where those designations appear in this book and
Adams Media was aware of a trademark claim, the designations have been printed
with initial capital letters.

This book is available at quantity discounts for bulk purchases.
For information, please call 1-800-872-5627.
Visit our home page at *www.adamsmedia.com*

Contents

IF YOU'RE AN INCORRIGIBLE PACK RAT, the mere thought of clutter control must seem a daunting task. You probably didn't set out to collect all of this clutter deliberately, yet somehow now, when you look around, you suddenly find yourself drowning in all of it. Your clutter problem is, most likely, one that has been building for years. It starts innocently enough, with little things, like letting old magazines pile up on the living room coffee table or pushing aside all of those old memos that tend to pile up on your desk. Before you know it, though, your house is a mess, your office is a mess, and your brain is so overloaded thinking about all of the different things you need to accomplish that you haven't a clue about how to cut your clutter short.

Once clutter spirals out of control, getting a handle on even a small piece of it, whether it be cleaning out the dreaded refrigerator or ridding yourself of all the unnecessary, outdated clothing that still occupies space in your closet, seems unlikely. That's only because you don't know where to start. Don't resign yourself to living in the midst of all your clutter. You really can find fast, easy ways to clean up your mess, and you really can conquer the chaos in all aspects of your life. You just need to know where to start and how to motivate yourself. Here's the secret: You don't need to launch a grandiose, full-scale assault on every inch of clutter in your life, all at once. Yes, eventually your goal should be to eradicate clutter in all its forms, but you can start small, and you can do it in steps.

An essential part of becoming a more organized, productive person means finding ways to deal with and eliminate not only physical, tangible clutter in your living and working space, but also clutter in its more abstract forms. Maybe you never thought about it, but schedule clutter, mental clutter, and emotional clutter are just as real as any other kind of clutter—and often more destructive. These things breed excess stress, cause you to procrastinate, prompt you to waste your time in unproductive ways, encourage you to cling to past memories and experiences unnecessarily, and even deflate your self-esteem.

Bet you had no idea. Don't worry; just read on, because this book is meant to serve as a step-by-step guide to help you through the process of clearing clutter from your life, once and for all. The sooner you learn how to unclutter all aspects of your life effectively, the sooner you'll be able to refocus your energies on the things that really matter to you. So stop allowing your clutter to shape your life, and start taking charge.

chapter 1

Slaying the Clutter Dragon

IT STARTS OUT RATHER INNOCENTLY—a few things you bought to decorate your home (or yourself)—just a few nice things, "must-haves" you couldn't pass up. Then a pattern begins—a few more bargains you couldn't refuse, a closet full of clothes you might still wear when you lose those last five pounds, an attic full of items you haven't seen in twenty years but insist on keeping . . . just in case you need them someday.

Before you know it, the mighty clutter dragon has reared its ugly head—and you begin to feel the fire breathing down your neck—usually in the form of a spouse or family member who starts telling you it's time to clean up your act.

You probably know that all of these people who are encouraging you to get rid of your clutter are right. After a long, stressful, busy day at work, when you're dying to come home to some peace, quiet, and comfort, the last thing you want to encounter is that pile of dirty laundry, mound of unwashed dishes, and stack of newspapers and magazines just waiting to be sorted through and recycled. Not to mention those footprints in the kitchen, and—oh, no—those videos you rented last week and were supposed to return yesterday. Suddenly, it seems impossible to get a handle on it all.

But coming home—or staying home all day—doesn't have to feel so overwhelming. It can be a relaxing, peaceful, or even exhilarating experience if you want it to be. It's your home. It can be what you make it, and it shouldn't be just one more great big stressful burden. If your home isn't the place you want it to be, you are probably in dire need of clutter control!

Simplify, Simplify

Chinese tradition says that the more things you own, the more problems you will have in life. Think about it: When you were in college and basically had nothing, wasn't life simpler, too? So many "live simpler" books have sold well in the last few years because we all seek a simpler life. Yet many of us still have basements, attics, and family rooms filled with clutter.

Western culture has placed such an emphasis on materialism that people believe they need more than they actually do. The need to have many things is particularly strong in American culture—and it can easily turn into a fixation that is difficult to overcome. Look at the success of eBay, which lists more than a million items for sale by their owners on a daily basis. That's a lot of stuff!

It's no wonder so many people have problems with excessive clutter when every day, they are inundated with more and more opportunities to buy things that will supposedly enhance their lives. The overwhelming accumulation of stuff just seems to happen. It becomes harder and harder to accept life as it is at this moment, without yielding to any of the infinite opportunities encountered daily to "improve" it. Practice saying "no" to things for one day, and you'll see what conscious effort it requires!

Curtail Your Shopping

Excessive shopping can be particularly bothersome in the quest for clutter control because it works in direct opposition to any efforts toward simplifying your life. Some people get a fantastic high from shopping, and shopping can, indeed, turn into an addiction. If you head to the store when you are feeling frustrated, depressed, anxious, or worried about something, because buying a bunch of new stuff makes you feel better, you are shopping for the wrong reason. You are also, no doubt, cluttering up your home with a ton of unnecessary things. We live in a consumption-crazed society, and we're encouraged from many different directions to buy things. But you should only buy things that you really need or want. That doesn't mean wanting to buy just "anything at all." Is the temporary excitement you get from toting home a new little treasure worth the mess you're left to deal with when your basement, attic, closets, and cupboards start overflowing with things you never wear, use, eat, or look at again?

■ ■ ■ ■ ■ Clutter Control Quickie: Become a Connoisseur

A little creativity can go a long way in turning a clutter habit into a worthwhile hobby. If you have a penchant for snapping up all sorts of knickknacks any time you go shopping, stop buying whatever you see and start collecting something valuable instead. Learn about early American ceramics, antique train sets, or cat or dog statues from around the world. Collect whatever strikes your fancy—just focus on that one collection and quit buying anything and everything! ■

Just like overeating—or any other bad habit, for that matter—the shopping habit *can* be redirected. If you think you shop for the wrong reasons, work on finding something else fun to do whenever the shopping bug bites. Something that doesn't cost any money is particularly smart. It might not feel as good at first, but once you get *out of the habit,* you'll wonder how you could possibly have spent so much money on so much junk. Remember, the best things in life aren't things!

When Your Cup Runneth Over

Before you get started on the road to fixing specific trouble spots, it might be a good idea to do a general clutter check. How can you tell if you've attained official pack-rat status? Look for these telltale signs.

- Your bookshelves are overstuffed receptacles for many things, only half of which are actually books.
- Your clothes overflow from your closet and land in piles on the floor, chair, treadmill, dressing table, or wherever else in sight.
- Your kitchen "junk" drawers are so full they don't even shut properly.
- Your pantries and cabinets are stuffed with food you no longer eat or like—or worse, don't even remember you have. (Think back to the last time you bought a new bottle of ketchup at the supermarket, only to find two more tucked way at the back of a shelf days later.)
- Your medicine chests are filled with old or expired medications.
- Your garage and attic are catch-alls full of stuff you have no place else to stash.
- Your desk is crammed with papers so old you can't remember what they're for anymore.
- You have a collection of useless, broken items you keep meaning to fix, when you have time.
- You're afraid to look under your bed; that's where you throw all the stuff you don't have space to store or time to deal with—because out of sight is out of mind.

As out of control as your clutter-filled life might seem, the reality is that you have much more control over your excesses than you think. Slaying the clutter dragon is possible—once you learn to have a new perspective, take a hard look at yourself, and honestly assess your life. Thankfully, there is a clutter cure—it's just not easy. You have to be determined to reorganize what you do need, rid yourself of what you don't, and then learn to say no to acquiring more useless things. (Because what good is it if you make a clean sweep, only to turn around and start filling your space with more useless stuff all over again?) Don't expect to achieve your new clutter-free goals all at once. Just like a twelve-step program, you'll have to take it one day—and one space—at a time.

Clutter Intangibles

The Chinese have a saying: A cluttered house is a cluttered mind. Before you dive into that cluttered house, office, garage—or what-ever other area of space that has become unbearably oppressive due to lack of organization or excessive mess—you first need to unclutter your mental and emotional space.

The most important thing about clearing clutter of all kinds is to recognize that it is necessary in order to wipe your energy slate clean, so to speak. You need to order your sur-roundings in the most positive, unaffected way possible—and clutter blocks good energy from flowing through your environment.

What Clutter Really Means

Although tiny living spaces, lack of storage areas, cramped work cubicles, and other physical limitations make it hard to stay mess-free, sometimes the biggest obstacles to clutter control are mental and emotional. Author Karen Kingston (*Clear Your Clutter with Feng Shui,* Broadway Books, 1999) says the process of clearing clutter from your environment is actually a process of releasing, and of letting go emotionally. When you begin to rid your home of clutter, you also begin to release old attachments to things that no longer serve you or bring you joy.

For instance, you might be keeping an old pair of tennis shoes that you wore on a favorite date, but since the relationship ultimately didn't work out, keeping those shoes amounts to hanging on to something that is no longer part of your life. Such tendencies can possibly hold you back from a rewarding new relationship because, psychologically speaking, you are holding on to the past.

When you begin to clear away years' worth of clutter from your attic, you might be amazed by how much stuff from your past has been holding you back from your future.

Fear and Hoarding

Don't underestimate the power of fear. It's a huge motivator when it comes to holding on to unnecessary things. As you walk through piles of old clothes, record albums, books, and knick-knacks, you might wonder why you've been keeping all of these things for so long. Did you expect to use them again one day? Not likely. Instead, you probably hadn't felt ready to relinquish your past due to your uncertainty regarding your future.

▦ ▦ ▦ ▦ ▦ Clutter Control Quickie: Do a Litmus Test

The best test for eliminating clutter is to look at each item and ask yourself, "When was the last time I used this?" If your answer is more than a year ago, it's probably not an essential item in your life and it might be of better use to someone else. ▦

Between going to college, changing jobs, repeatedly moving, or coping with the various stages of marriage, the possibility of not having enough to survive is a very real concern. Transitions are often tough to make, and when you're in a state of continual change it's easy to take comfort in emotional hoarding, collecting things to pacify a soul that is yearning for love, security, or other types of satisfaction that money can't buy. If you fit this bill, you probably never even realized what you were doing—until you turned around one day to find you had so much stuff in your home you could hardly breathe! In order to clear your life of clutter, you need to purge yourself of all the items that no longer serve you.

As you take a deeper look into the psychological ties you've had to the past, don't forget to think about *all* of the clutter traps in your life. Think about clutter in the garage, basement, hall closet, and even in your car! If you look more deeply at the situation, you can learn lots of interesting things about your clutter patterns. If, for instance, you are a real homebody and have barricaded yourself into your garage with clutter, maybe it's time to consider starting a home-based business instead, so you can spend more time at home—in a healthier manner.

The key to dealing with clutter is being able to read into your needs and your motivations in order to find out why you are keeping what you are keeping. Once you understand your motivations, you can eliminate the clutter for good—and greatly improve your inner sense of well-being.

Environment as Metaphor

According to feng shui, the ancient Chinese art of placement, our environment is a metaphor for our lives and the energy that comes and goes in our lives. Quite simply, problems in your environment mean problems in your life.

Consider this for a moment. If your home is a metaphor for your life, how does your life look? Take a good look around. Is your life cluttered with stuff you don't need? How's the circulation? How long has it been since you've done preventive maintenance on your life?

Your office, either at home or at your work away from home, can also be a metaphor for your life. Is your life scattered with unpaid bills, things to file, scraps of information that take up energy but don't give anything back, malfunctioning equipment, unstable piles of books, files, binders, and folders?

If what you find in your home or office space is not exactly what you have in mind for your life, it's time to take matters in hand. Let your home and office continue to be a metaphor for your life, but shape that metaphor in a way that suits you. Keep it clean, get rid of the clutter, and create a relaxing, positive atmosphere where you can decompress and feel happy at the end of each day.

Once you've gotten into the habit of keeping your house in order, you'll find how calming and rejuvenating it is to be in your home. Then, whenever things start to get out of order again, train yourself to recognize the immediate and visible clues that indicate clutter is creeping into your life again, and stop it.

Making More Space

Some people feel comforted by a room full of stuff, but there is something relaxing and calming about a clean, clutter-free surface, a wall with a single hanging, an expanse of carpet without any toys, books, or discarded clothes, even a room with just a few basic pieces of necessary furniture. While not everyone likes to live in a home that is completely minimal and utilitarian, chances are that over the years, your home has accumulated a couple of layers of decor.

If so, it's time to put away, give away, or just plain throw out some of that stuff in order to free up space. As you make space on your surfaces, floors, walls, and rooms, you'll feel like you are making space in your mind. You'll also feel more relaxed and calmer in that clean, organized, uncluttered space. If you donate stuff, you'll get the added sense of satisfaction that comes from helping others. Or, if you sell on consignment, you can make a little pocket money.

Living in a Small Space

If you live in a studio apartment, college dorm room, or even a small house, space is a huge premium. Most likely, you have to use every room or area of your home for multiple purposes. For example, your living area may double as your home office, guest room, and dining area. Your kitchen may also serve as your laundry area, and your bedroom may provide the majority of your storage space, in addition to being a place to sleep.

If your living space is small, be especially aware of the areas where clutter tends to creep in, and then be sure to utilize every possible inch of unused space you do have for storage. Pay special attention to the various storage ideas presented throughout this book and experiment with them so you make them work in your space. Make the most of under-bed storage, add extra shelving wherever there is room to do so, maximize the use of floor and wall space (and even the ceiling), and think in terms of using multipurpose furniture. For example, by putting cushions on top of a sturdy wooden storage chest, you can create a comfortable seat or bench, but that same bench can pull double duty as a storage spot to organize various items that might otherwise cramp your quarters if left out in the open.

■ ■ ■ ■ ■ Clutter Control Quickie: Strategic Shelving

Keep your books organized and off the floor by building special shelves onto walls in different rooms of your house, such as one in your kitchen for cookbooks. To save even more floor space, consider using taller, narrower bookcases. Place your most commonly used items at eye-level for easy reference and your least used items higher up. Don't forget to organize the books, CDs, DVDs, software, and videos on your shelves by author, title, or subject. ■

When you're forced to live in a small space, fully utilizing your closets is critical, so pay particular attention to the chapter on closets, which explores a wide range of closet organizing options and tools. For instance, if your closet is tall, you can install additional upper shelves, to store seasonal items, such as blankets, boots, and heavy sweaters. Also, determine whether you can install a double row of clothing rods. Slacks and long coats need full-height vertical space, but you might be able to double up on suits, jackets, shirts and blouses. By adding that second row of space, you'll save yourself from stuffing too much onto a single rack in a cluttered, crowded closet.

Reduce Clutter, Reduce Stress

Clutter does more than keep your home, your desk, or your garage looking messy. It keeps your mind messy, too. The more stuff you have—especially if it's disorganized, unmatched, lost, or high-maintenance stuff—the more you have to worry about finding it, maintaining it, keeping it, and dealing with it. Getting rid of the clutter in your home is the most important thing you can do to make your home a stress-free haven of tranquility.

Don't worry—clutter control doesn't have to mean getting rid of everything. If you love your things and love to be surrounded by them, the trick to staving off clutter and having a stress-free living environment is keeping your things well organized. If everything is kept neat and you know where it all is, then your favorite things can bring you as much joy, comfort, and calm as a sparser space.

chapter 2

Uncluttering Your Schedule

OKAY, YOU UNDERSTAND THE EFFECT past emotional baggage can have on your tendency to be a pack rat, so you're ready to get rid of the clutter in your kitchen, living room, bedroom, attic, garage, and basement, right? Not necessarily. There are other kinds of clutter that also impede the clearing of physical clutter—and though they are not as obvious, they can still create obstacles in your life.

You want to maximize the power of organization to create a more comfortable living environment, but in order to do this, you need to understand how to manage your time effectively so you can boost productivity. After all, a crazy, haphazard schedule can be a major obstacle to clutter control. If you're always busy rushing breathlessly from one task to another, you probably don't have the time to figure out how to best organize yourself or your space. That's when junk starts getting stuffed into closets, shoved under beds, or piled high on desks. Once you learn how to make the best use of your time, you'll reduce your stress level, free up mental space, and have more energy to focus on reorganization projects.

Organizing Your Morning

Every morning you wake up to the same basic routine—you're tired, you're running late, you can't figure out what you're going to wear, you can't find your car keys, and you still have half a dozen other things to do when you realize, on top of it all, you forgot to recharge your cell phone last night. While you probably can't change most of the things you have to do every day, you can take a more organized approach so that your mornings are less stressful. When your morning goes smoothly, you'll set the stage for the rest of the day.

First, consider what time you need to leave for work and think about all the activities involved in your morning routine. Make a complete list, preferably in order, starting from the moment you wake up in the morning. Include the time it takes to brush your teeth, shower, iron your clothes, shave, put on your makeup, do your hair, or make the bed. If you brew coffee, eat breakfast, or exercise before you leave, figure that in, too. Now write down approximately how long each task takes. Also try to predict other things that come up in the course of the morning to slow you down—like scraping some unexpected frost off your car before you leave—and allow yourself some extra time for those things.

With all of this in mind, do the math and figure out exactly when you need to wake up to ensure you'll be on time. Then set your alarm clock and stick to it (that means no hitting the snooze button). To keep yourself on schedule in the morning, make sure clocks are easily visible in the bedroom, bathroom, and kitchen.

▨ ▨ ▨ ▨ ▨ Clutter Control Quickie: Group Your Morning Must-Haves

To make things easier while you're getting ready in the morning, organize your bathroom to accommodate your daily routine. Create a sublist of everything you do in the bathroom and what items you need for shaving, applying makeup, styling your hair, taking a shower, and so on. Create separate areas for each of these activities and group items for each activity together. Or use small, portable storage bins and trays, to keep your shaving stuff apart from your hair-care products, for example. ▨

Once you fully understand what you need to accomplish each morning, you can devise more effective ways to tackle these activities more quickly, and even multitask, so you reduce your early-morning stress. Start the coffee machine *before* you get in the shower, or warm up the iron while you're choosing your clothes, and you'll save yourself time.

Often, a lot of the things that cause stress first thing in the morning can be avoided altogether, just by doing them the night before. It's much easier to get in the habit of spending twenty or thirty minutes before bedtime to get your clothes ready, make lunches, locate your car keys and cell phone, and pack your briefcase so you're ready to go.

■ ■ ■ ■ Clutter Control Quickie: Streamline Your Breakfast Routine

If you make coffee or breakfast in the morning, instead of randomly rifling through various kitchen drawers, figure out exactly what you need, and keep those items in one specific, convenient area of the kitchen. Store opened breakfast condiments, such as honey, jelly, and syrup in a small container or basket in the refrigerator, so you can find them all at once. ■

Outfit Organizers

If you're often fumbling for the things you need to get dressed each morning, consider buying a hardwood valet to hang and organize your outfit the night before, so everything is ready and wrinkle-free. The Frontgate catalog (888-263-9850, *www.frontgate.com*) sells the Hardwood Gentleman's Valet, which has hanging space for a complete business suit, small drawers for change or cufflinks, a shelf for your other accessories, hooks for a belt and tie, and a built-in shoe rack. There are also smaller dresser-top valets with multiple compartments or drawers for organizing your glasses, jewelry, watch, wallet, keys, pens, PDA, and pager. It definitely beats digging through dresser drawers or cluttered countertops.

Capitalizing on Your Commuting Time

No matter where you live, if you commute to work by car, one of the things you'll probably have to deal with on a regular basis is heavy traffic. Instead of boiling over with road rage, make commuting time more productive and relaxing.

The radio is great for keeping track of the news or listening to music, and if you have a cassette or CD player, you can listen to audio tapes of all those how-to books or novels you just can't seem to find the time to read. (You know, the ones piled in stacks that clutter up your living room floor.) But if you don't want to spend your time just listening to someone else speak, do the talking yourself. Use your cell or digital PCS phone to check voice mail, return important phone calls, chat with friends and loved ones, or even hold business meetings via conference calls. (Just make sure to use a headset or speakerphone so that your driving isn't distracted!)

▪ ▪ ▪ ▪ ▪ Clutter Control Quickie: Organize Vitamins and Medicine

Save yourself time and effort by getting any vitamins or medicine you need to take daily at night. Then leave them in an accessible place where you can easily grab them in the morning. If you stick to a routine, you won't worry about missing a dose. ▪

If you're not the one doing the driving and instead carpool, take the train, or use some other form of public transportation to get to work, you have even more opportunity for organizing yourself during your commute. Plan your daily schedule, surf the Web (using a wireless modem and a laptop or a wireless PDA), or sneak in a little extra work so you won't have to do it at home. Take care of these nitty-gritty essentials during your commute, and you won't be distracted by them when you get home. Then you'll have more free time to stay on top of clutter control.

▪ ▪ ▪ ▪ ▪ Clutter Control Quickie: Talk on Tape

If you're feeling time-deprived because of your commute, try using a microcassette recorder while sitting in traffic. Lots of people boost their overall productivity and organize their day this way by dictating letters and memos, keeping track of ideas when they can't write them down, and reciting a daily to-do list on their way to and from work. ▪

Taking Control of the Rest of Your Day

You probably spend at least eight hours a day, five days a week, on the job. This leaves nights and weekends to juggle personal responsibilities as well as time with friends and family. By the time you're finished with all your professional and personal responsibilities, there's probably little or no time left for you. Believe it or not, you can unclutter your schedule if you look at it more closely and learn how to organize it better.

Just as you did with your morning routine, the first step is determining exactly how you're spending every minute of your day right now. That might sound daunting at first, but just grab a calendar or a blank sheet of paper, and think about two or three typical weekdays and at least one full weekend. Create a detailed diary of how you spend your time, from essentials like sleeping, cooking, eating, driving, reading mail, paying bills, running errands, and attending meetings, to down-time activities like visiting with friends and family, watching television, reading, shopping, or doing other hobbies. Now calculate how much time you spend on each important task—and how much time you waste on unimportant things.

■ ■ ■ ■ ■ Clutter Control Quickie: Order Your Essentials

Find yourself frantically searching for your keys every day? Carve out a spot near your front door to organize essential items. Use a small shelf or board with hooks to hold keys, outgoing mail, shopping lists, cell phone, and other items you tend to lose track of every day. Put your keys on this hook or shelf every time you come home, and remember to plug your cell phone into its charger and keep it near your keys. ■

When you see your schedule laid out before you in detail, it's easier to pinpoint some of the ongoing activities that take up time unnecessarily. Again, you can probably come up with ways to combine tasks in order to save time, and you can probably cut down on a lot of time wasters. You can also determine the times of the day when you're the most productive, isolate the aspects of your life that cause you the most stress, and make other adjustments that allow you to use your time to your best ability.

Be On Time

Perennial lateness is a particularly bothersome form of intangible clutter that can wreck your time management and cause loads of stress. If you're always late, think about why. Are you perpetually disorganized? Do you like the power that comes from making people wait for you? You probably have plenty of excuses: You were "running behind." You have "too much on your plate." You "didn't think." But these are only excuses; you do have control over these things.

The bottom line is, being late all the time is inconsiderate and rude. It makes you look bad, and it sets a bad example for the people who look up to you—especially your children. If you have this problem, tackling tardiness should be your first order of business. Start getting ready for anything you have to do about an hour ahead of time and make sure you have everything you need well before you need it. That means deciding what you are going to wear and digging the right shoes out of the closet in advance!

Learning to Prioritize

Now that you've learned a bit about helping to move your day-to-day activities along more smoothly, it's time to look more closely at strategies to reduce mental clutter and keep time running smoothly in the long term. This involves learning how to prioritize, acknowledging the difference between important and urgent tasks, recognizing when you need to shift your focus, mastering the art of the to-do list, creating a workable schedule, realizing your limitations, and staying on top of your time management. Sounds like a lot, doesn't it? Don't worry, once you get in the groove of things, your system will take over. Soon, it will feel as if you're running on autopilot, and your clutter control routine will start rolling along!

Before you do anything else, you need to set your priorities. That means figuring out what's most important to you. Although you have different sets of priorities at work than you have at home, look at your life in general at first. Brainstorm about everything that is important to you. Your list might be long, or it might have only a few key items. Either way is fine, just be honest with yourself. Once you have your list, pull out the top ten items that are most significant to you, and rank them accordingly. Don't toss the rest; you might want to use them later for other sublists or to re-evaluate this starter list. This list is by no means set in stone. Don't be afraid to make changes—you'll be continually reevaluating and restructuring as you go along.

A Pressing Matter

Too many people—usually those who manage time poorly—consider nearly everything they do during the day to be urgent. Although the words "important" and "urgent" are often used interchangeably, they do mean different things. Something is "Important" if it has value or significance; something is "Urgent" if it calls for immediate attention. In order to prioritize correctly and get a handle on the things in life that matter to you, you need to recognize the difference.

It's impossible to make decisions regarding what and when tasks should be done if everything demands attention right away. How can you even think about finding the time to reorganize that mess in the living room if your cell phone is constantly ringing, the computer is shooting off reminders that you have mail, you are late taking your kids to school, and your dog is whining to go out? When simply making it through the course of your day feels this hectic and cluttered, you don't think, you just react.

▪ ▪ ▪ ▪ ▪ Clutter Control Quickie: Just Say No

Learn to say no to requests that don't add up to time well spent for you. You don't have to be on every single committee that comes your way. You don't have to join lots of different clubs. Cut out unnecessary things, and you'll have more time and energy to focus on the things that count. If you've already taken on too much, start purging. Don't let anything waste your time! ▪

Important matters will have the greatest influence on your life, but they are often pushed aside in favor of urgent ones. Those things considered most important vary from person to person, but it all comes down to what you personally consider meaningful. It's easy to get caught up in urgency mode and disregard all other tasks. That's when you get stuck in a vicious cycle of chaos—when important tasks are disregarded long enough, they eventually work their way into the urgent category.

Those cell phone calls and e-mail messages will always be there; they can wait. If your lack of control over your cluttered life is driving you nuts and compromising your sense of happiness and well-being, you've got to tune out those seemingly "urgent," incessant disruptions and carve out the time for the important tasks.

Shifting Focus

So how do you break the cycle? First, you need to divide your activities into four categories to get a good look at what emphasis you place on each. The first category should include those activities that are both urgent and important. These should take precedence over everything else. This includes stuff like getting your squeaky brakes checked or finishing that important report at work on time. The second category is comprised of those activities that are important but not urgent, such as getting a regular physical exam; discussing upcoming vacation time with your family; or sorting and paying your bills.

The third category is made up of activities that are urgent but not important. This can be the troublesome classification. Urgency wants to scream importance, but on careful examination, most of these urgent matters hold little long-term value. Speeding for fear of being late for something or running to the nearest pay phone to answer a page from someone whose number you don't even recognize probably aren't all that impactful.

The last category is the not-urgent and not-important division. This is the fun stuff—watching television, catching up with friends, or beating that new video game. If you feel overwhelmed with the urgencies, try avoiding this last category for a few days to free up time and take care of what needs to be done.

Ultimately, all of this prioritizing and time management is about honing your focus because, if you're having time troubles, chances are you lost your focus somewhere along the line. Or, perhaps you can still see what is important, but it's a bit blurred. As soon as you lose focus on the important things in life, you lose the ability to make calculated decisions, to achieve goals, and to enjoy yourself overall.

Shifting focus is not easy. Once you make the shift, you might not accomplish as many tasks as you did beforehand, and you'll probably have to stop jumping on every little thing that comes up each day. Keep in mind that it isn't the quantity but the quality that matters.

Setting Goals

Lack of organization and planning are often why so many people never seem to have time in the day to accomplish their goals. One way to begin taking control of your life (and your time) is to set detailed short- and long-term goals for yourself. Label separate sheets of paper "Daily," "Weekly," or "Monthly," or whatever time frame you feel specific tasks should be accomplished. If you want to reorganize your garage, for instance, exactly what needs to be done? Do you need to clean out, put things on shelves or in cabinets, or simply free up some space so you can actually fit your car inside for a change?

Once you figure that out, set time limits. This is just as important as the goal itself. Without time limits, you have no way of knowing when you should work on a project or when it should be completed. For immediate tasks, try to set the time limit as precisely as possible. For longer-term goals, you might need to define the time frame more loosely. But always try to get as close as you can. You might be motivated to complete the project, but if there isn't a deadline, it is easy to push it aside to make room for something else. Don't allow this to happen. Be as strict with yourself as possible when it comes to your goals.

Define the Steps

Once you have a precisely defined goal in front of you, break it down into steps. Set time limits to these as well and you'll reach your end goal smoothly and quickly. These mini goals are stepping stones that act as stimulants. The further you break down a goal, the better you'll be able to see the light at the end of the tunnel, and the easier it will seem to achieve.

Remember, you have to be realistic in your expectations, or else you'll end up disappointed and discouraged when you don't accomplish as much as quickly as you thought you would. Set your standards high, just not out of reach.

People who are successful have almost always mastered the ability to set goals and plan, and they typically have strong time-management and organizational techniques. Take time to consider what is (or what you want to be) truly important in your life, then outline steps to get there.

Create a To-Do List

A to-do list is an invaluable tool in the quest for clutter control. It allows you to plan ahead and enables you to take charge of your time without feeling overwhelmed. To-do lists lend a sense of order to your life, so you're able to eagerly, not anxiously, anticipate the day ahead of you. And let's face it, in the hustle and bustle of our everyday lives, it is easy to overlook an important task. Decision-making processes are easier with a to-do list, and it can also be a great motivator, because you get to cross off every task you accomplish. This leaves you with a feeling of success, which can be very encouraging.

▨ ▨ ▨ ▨ ▨ Clutter Control Quickie: Stay Realistic

Successful to-do lists are simple, realistic, and accessible. If you can't complete even a fraction of the tasks on your list, you'll become upset and frustrated with yourself. That won't help you to be productive. In fact, if you are constantly stressed out, rushing to complete each task, it will probably only make your life more hectic. Don't become a slave to your list! ▨

Every evening (after work) or first thing in the morning, take about fifteen minutes to create a daily to-do list for yourself. List all of your prescheduled appointments in your daily schedule, allowing ample time to get to and from the appointments, and if necessary, allocating time to prepare for them in advance. Along with your appointments, add any other little tasks you have to get done.

Now, set your priorities. Put an "A" next to tasks that will produce the most valuable results—the items that must get done, no matter what. Then, place a "B" next to important tasks you need to accomplish, but aren't as critical or time-sensitive. Finally, put a "C" next to items that should get done, but that aren't immediately important. Give the high-priority items your full attention and attempt to complete them early in the day. Keep in mind that urgent tasks have short-term consequences, but tasks that you determine will have long-term implications help you to reach your goals.

By applying time-management and organization skills to everything you do, you'll find your life will become less stressful as you become more productive. Taking advantage of the time-management and organization tools available to you will also help you to better achieve your clutter-control goals.

Basic Time Management Tools

There are some basic tools you'll want to have if you're serious about uncluttering your time. First of all, you'll need a calendar. There are lots to choose from, but consider your needs. Do you need it just to show the date, or are you planning to mark appointments on it? Do you want a big one you can see across the room or a small one to fit in your purse? Also consider where you want to place it.

Though you might find you need more than one calendar, don't use more than one for your appointments. If you have appointments scattered on various calendars, it's a sure shot you'll miss something.

▪ ▪ ▪ ▪ ▪ Clutter Control Quickie: Use a Family Calendar

Using one calendar for the entire family efficiently keeps everyone's schedule uncluttered. Keep it in the kitchen or some other high-traffic zone, and encourage your family to mark down all upcoming activities and appointments. This is a good way to keep tabs on things so everyone knows what is going on in each other's lives. ▪

Invest in a daily planner, but don't let the fancy ones suck you in if you only plan to use it as an appointment book. Consider the convenience of the sections offered. For example, several planners come equipped with blank pages for notes; pages for shopping lists, to-do lists, and check lists; an address book; a telephone book; a personal budget; a month-by-month calendar; weekly spreads; maps; emergency information; and even calculators. If you will actually use all this stuff, fantastic. If not, weed out unnecessary sections.

Also consider creating your own planner. It can be as simple as a spiral-bound notebook or as elaborate as a customized leather-bound book with a table of contents leading to color-coded sections. The choice is yours. But do keep in mind that for this to work effectively, it must be portable, updated frequently, and organized.

The Frills

Okay, forget the basics. Now it's time to move on to the frills. Electronic organizers such as PalmPilot, Sharp Wizard, and BlackBerry Handheld make paper seem obsolete. These handy little contraptions bring the power of your computer to the palm of your hand. You can organize; set appointments; store addresses, phone numbers, and to-do lists; track your time; and make changes quickly and easily. What's not to love?

▩ ▩ ▩ ▩ ▩ Clutter Control Quickie: Stay Ahead of the Game

It's always a good idea to plan your schedule ahead of time. Don't try to sit down hour by hour and figure out what you need to do. Look over your schedule the night before to make any necessary changes and prepare yourself for the day ahead. Also remember not to get so swept up in your day-to-day activities that you forget to add in your long-term goals. ▩

Before you take the plunge into technology, be sure you're ready. If you aren't familiar with these products, it will take a bit of time to research and find what best suits your needs, not to mention the time it will take to learn the programs. Also keep in mind that electronic organizers can be expensive and can break, so it's important to back up your data. And don't let all those cool features distract you from your clutter-control mission!

Keeping a Firm Handle on Your Time

Based on the priorities and goals you've set and the tasks you need to accomplish each day on the to-do lists you're now creating, what needs to change in order to reduce your time clutter? How can you modify your habits so you spend more time being productive and less time being stressed out? According to the Day Timer's 4-Dimensional Time Management program, a course that teaches time-management skills, to manage your time successfully, you must keep the following points in mind:

- **Focus:** Determine which duties you're responsible to perform in a timely manner, and learn to differentiate between what's important and what's not.
- **Plan:** Discover how to prioritize the items on your to-do list properly. Establish tasks based on your goals and decide in advance how much time each task will take.
- **Act:** Based on your planning, take an organized approach to completing each of the high-priority tasks and items on your to-do list every day. Focus on the less important items and tasks later.

Good time management requires constant maintenance. You will have to reorganize your priorities, reevaluate your goals, and update your schedule on a regular basis. However, the monthly, annual, and lifetime goals have a way of fading from the picture for long periods of time and then sneaking up on you suddenly. Don't let this happen. Stay on top of them so they don't get out of control.

chapter 3

Recognizing and Coping with Stress

MAKING IT THROUGH DAY-TO-DAY LIFE while your schedule is hectic and you're surrounded by excess clutter certainly causes undue stress. But the reverse scenario is also true: Any type of stress can clutter your mind and interfere with your ability to accomplish things productively. Anything out of the ordinary that happens to you is stressful on your body. Some of that stress feels good, or even great. Stress isn't necessarily bad—without any stress at all, life would be terribly boring. But stress certainly isn't always good, either. It can cause dramatic problems in your life if you have too much of it and for too long.

Often, when we think about stress, we think about big things—like unexpectedly losing a job or dealing with a health crisis. Stress can also be more subtle, hidden, and deeply imbedded, however. Even when you're used to certain things in your life—dirty dishes in the sink, family members who don't help you out, twelve-hour days at the office, where the work just seems to pile higher and higher—it can still be very stressful. You might actually be accustomed to all of the clutter in your life, in spite of the stress it causes. When clutter becomes this routine and familiar, it's even tougher to break. It might even feel weird or uncomfortable to think of your home being too clean! You are so used to things the way they are, you can't imagine how to adjust.

Types of Stress

Most people have a preconceived notion of what stress means—worry, anxiety, excitement, fear, or uncertainty. These things cause people stress and are mostly conditions stemming from stress. Stress comes in several guises, some more obvious than others.

When Life Changes: Acute Stress

Acute stress is the most obvious. It's easy to spot if you associate it with one thing: change. You know how this works—stuff you're not used to almost always causes stress. Acute stress can develop from any sort of change: from a change in your diet or exercise routine, to a change in your job or the people involved in your life, whether you've lost them or gained them. You get used to things being a certain way, physically, mentally, emotionally, even chemically, then something comes along and disturbs your body's equilibrium, and *voila*—acute stress creeps in.

▪ ▪ ▪ ▪ ▪ Clutter Control Quickie: Mind Your Mental Clutter

Mental clutter happens when you allow your brain to fill with thoughts, worries, and concerns about the future—or past. To alleviate this kind of clutter, consider journaling. It's a positive, healthy way to get worries and other forms of mental clutter out of your mind and into a safe, directed place. ▪

Acute stress is hard on our bodies and our minds because people tend to be creatures of habit. Even the most spontaneous and schedule-resistant among us have our habits, and habits don't just mean enjoying that morning cup of coffee or sleeping on that favorite side of the bed. Habits include minute, complex, intricate interworkings of physical, chemical, and emotional factors on our bodies. This doesn't mean that you should avoid all change. Everyone needs a certain degree of change. But here's the tricky part: How much change you can stand before the changes have a negative effect on you is a completely individual issue. No single formula can calculate what "too much stress" is for any one person because it varies.

When Life Is a Roller Coaster: Episodic Stress

Episodic stress is like lots of acute stress—in other words, lots of life changes—all at once and over a period of time. People who suffer from episodic stress always seem to be in the midst of some tragedy. They tend to be overwrought, sometimes intense, and often irritable, angry, or anxious.

If you've ever been through a week, a month, even a year's worth of one personal disaster after another, you know what it's like to be in the throes of episodic stress. Episodic stress, like acute stress, can also come in more positive forms. For instance, experiencing the thrill of a whirlwind courtship, having a huge wedding, taking a honeymoon in Bali, buying a new home, and moving in with your new spouse for the first time, all in the same year, is an incredibly stressful sequence of events! Fun, sure. Romantic, yes. But it's still an excellent example of episodic stress.

Sometimes, episodic stress comes in a more subtle form—such as "worry." Worry is like inventing stress, or change, before it happens, even when it has little chance of happening. It saps the body's energy, usually for no good reason.

Worry doesn't solve problems. It's usually just the contemplation of horrible things that are unlikely to happen. It puts your body under stress by creating or imagining changes in the equilibrium of life—changes that haven't even happened! Worry takes up tons of mental space. If you can't unclutter your own brain, how are you ever going to unclutter the rest of your life?

When Life Stinks: Chronic Stress

Chronic stress is a different story. It has nothing to do with change—it's long-term, constant, unrelenting stress on the body, mind, or spirit. For example, someone living in poverty for years and years is under chronic stress. So is someone with a chronic, painful illness such as arthritis or migraine headaches. Living in a dysfunctional family or working at a job you hate is a source of chronic stress. So is low self-esteem.

This is all very heavy, serious stuff. Granted, there's no comparison between feeling trapped in an abusive relationship and feeling overwrought by all of your mental, emotional, or physical clutter. But the effects of chronic stress can be felt nonetheless. If left unchecked for too long, the disarray will become oppressive, and it will erode your energy and stilt your progress. The problem with chronic stress, whatever the source, is that people can't see how to get out of the situation. They come to believe life is supposed to be painful, stressful, or miserable. This can lead to depression, anxiety, or even physical, mental, or emotional breakdown.

The Effects of Mental Stress

We have lots of ways to describe our feelings of stress. Keyed up, wound up, geared up, fired up—all these expressions contain the word *up* because the stress response is, indeed, an "up" kind of experience. Muscles are pumped for action, senses are heightened, and awareness is sharpened. These feelings are useful, until they become too frequent. You might not think that functioning on a jumbled, hectic schedule, living in a messy, disorganized home, and working at an office that's in disarray is hazardous to your health, but the stress it puts on your body is very real if you get so worked up and irritated by all of this disaster that your blood pressure rises, your muscles tense, and your heart beats faster.

Stress causes your cerebral cortex to begin a process that results in the release of chemicals to prepare your body to handle danger. But what else goes on in your brain when you are under too much stress? Initially, you think more clearly and respond more quickly. But after you've reached your stress tolerance max, your brain begins to malfunction. This is when you reach the point of diminishing returns: You forget things. You lose things. You can't concentrate. You can't get anything done. To keep your brain working at its optimal level on a daily basis, you can't allow stress to clutter up your mental space and overwhelm your circuits!

Working too hard, pushing yourself too far, spreading yourself too thin, taking on too much, or living in a state of unhappiness or anxiety is incredibly stressful. Like physical stress, mental stress makes life difficult, and the harder things are, the more stress they cause. It's incredibly stressful when you feel like you can't get a handle on things, and if you delay dealing with the problems, things only get worse.

Just say you're staring at a stack of projects a mile high. Because of you're frantic pace, you can't fathom finding the time to do it all. So instead of stopping to unclutter your mind, your schedule, or your plan of attack, you throw yourself full force into your job, working endlessly and picking up all sorts of additional projects. This haphazard approach to work adds more stress to your life, as do the long hours, the lost sleep, and the poor dietary habits you've developed because of it. Your body begins to suffer, and so does your mind. Eventually, when you're juggling one too many projects, you will lose your perspective. That's when you become extra emotional or irritable—or both. You'll start to second guess your work performance and yourself in general, and frustration, anxiety, panic, or depression will set in.

■ ■ ■ ■ ■ Clutter Control Quickie: More Tips for Mental Clutter

If you don't always have enough time to journal, also try filling a "Thoughts and Worries" jar with concerns that you write on little slips of paper. This way, you'll give your anxiety—a.k.a. mental clutter—another place to live. When you leave your preoccupations in the pages of your journal or in a jar, you won't be as likely to carry them with you all through the day. ■

Mental stress can result in low self-esteem, a negative outlook on life, cynicism, or the desire for isolation, as the mind attempts to justify and, in any way possible, stop the stress. If you've ever had an extremely stressful week and want nothing more than to spend the entire weekend alone in bed with a good book and the remote control, you've experienced the mind attempting to regain its equilibrium. Too much activity and change can create a desire for zero activity and reversion to comfortable, familiar rituals.

Mental stress can be insidious because you can ignore it more easily than a physical illness. Yet, it is just as powerful and just as harmful to the body and to your life. If you allow stress to continue for too long, you could burn out and lose all interest in your tasks as your lack of control increases. You could even experience panic attacks, become depressed, or have a nervous breakdown. Ferreting out sources of mental stress is important to managing your time, your life, and your surroundings.

Stress and Your Self-Esteem

The intricate connection between stress and self-esteem can eat away at your motivation, productivity, and ability to initiate change in your life and your surroundings. Imagine that you've had a stressful day, one where everything goes wrong. (If you're in need of clutter control in all aspects of your life, you probably don't have to imagine!) First, you smack your shin on the bottom step as you leave for work. Then you spill coffee on your jacket before you even make it to your car—which refuses to start. At work, your boss dumps a project on you that will make the next two months a nightmare—you see many long nights ahead. You have to miss lunch because you're swamped, and your stress level is so obvious, a colleague tells you that you "look terrible." When you get home at the end of the day, you scrap your plans to go to the gym and then clean up the house and instead order a pizza and eat the whole thing. Naturally, you feel bad about skipping your exercise, giving in to junk food, eating way too much, and neglecting to get anything done. You feel so guilty that you make yourself an ice cream sundae and stay up late watching TV. By that point, you really have no energy left, so forget the dishes.

In the morning, you wake up puffy and your energy is drained. A messy kitchen greets you, you go to work exhausted, and you start the same stress routine you had the day before.

This cycle just continues. You keep overeating, undersleeping, and not doing anything about the things that are causing your stress, whatever they are—maybe because you don't have the energy and maybe because things have slipped so far you have no idea how to get a handle on them. You begin to feel worse and worse about yourself because you are so tired and so overwhelmed. The worse you feel about yourself, the more likely you are to continue your destructive patterns.

This kind of stress can really knock your sense of self-satisfaction for a loop. If your life is so stressful and your schedule so cluttered that you don't have any personal time, it's easy to feel like everything and everyone else matters more than you. You need to figure out how to jump in and slam on the brakes!

Fighting Stress by Focusing Your Energy

The first step in breaking the cycle is isolating one thing you can do something about. This will get you started and help you to focus. If you are overwhelmed because you have so many things going on in your life, you probably know what it is like to wander around in a daze, unable to concentrate on or accomplish any of them. Once you choose that thing you can do something about, don't allow yourself to be tempted by distraction! Yes, lots of other things need finishing, but they're never going to get done if you keep feeding your own mental clutter and disorganization by jumping from one task to the next.

▨ ▨ ▨ ▨ ▨ Clutter Control Quickie: Keep a Spending Journal

Financial clutter is largely a product of not knowing, wondering, hoping, fearing—because you have no idea what your money is actually doing. For at least a week or two, keep track of how you spend your money. Based on that knowledge, you can make a realistic budget that works. If you know exactly where your money is going, you won't have to waste time or energy fretting about it, and that will be a huge relief. ▨

The way you choose to focus is up to you. It might require getting one necessary task accomplished *all the way*. Or, it might involve some enforced personal time. The important thing is getting yourself centered again.

None of these strategies take more than thirty minutes, so you don't have any excuse not to do them. Anybody can spare thirty minutes out of a busy day in the name of feeling better and becoming more efficient, so get going!

Clean Your Kitchen Sink

If you are sick of your messy, cluttered home, but are so overwhelmed you don't know where to start, this is the remedy for you. Go to *www.flylady.net*, sign up for the daily reminders, and read everything on the site. This Web site contains a complete system for getting your house—and, by association, your life—in order, even if you've never been able to do it before. Be prepared to tow the mark, though. Flylady has a few ground rules and allows no whining about them. Flylady rule number one is to keep your kitchen sink empty, clean, and sparkling.

This might sound trivial if you're stuck in a rut pondering the remedy for other, seemingly more important disaster zones in your house. But this trick really does work—a clean sink has incredible stress-relieving power. In Flylady words, "As the kitchen goes, so goes the rest of the house." And, by extension, so does the rest of your life. The kitchen is the heart and soul of your house, and if your house is symbolic of your life (as it is in *feng shui),* then keeping the heart and soul in perfect order will resonate all over your life.

The kitchen is a ready-made springboard for jumping out of the stress cycle. No matter how busy, behind, or overwhelmed you are, if you take just thirty minutes—or even fifteen—to go into your kitchen, unload the clean dishes from the dishwasher and put them away, load up the dishwasher with the dirty ones, scrub the things you need to wash by hand, and then scrub down the sink when you're done, you won't believe the impact it will have on your self-esteem and motivation level. Once you have a pristine, sparkling sink, you just might feel the motivation to move onto other things!

Choose Another Chore

If you can make it past the kitchen sink, move on to another chore, and complete it. You'll get a feeling of accomplishment you could never get from half-finishing twenty different chores. None of these chores takes very long, but they are all things that many people have a hard time getting around to. When they remain undone, they weigh on your mind, add to your stress, and make you feel like you can't keep things under control. Doing just one thing on this list each day can make a huge difference in your feeling of accomplishment.

• **Clean out your car.** Throw out all the trash, return the recyclables, bring things back into the house, and attack those floor mats with the hand vac. Then, wipe down the windows with glass cleaner.

• **Clean out your purse or wallet.** Throw away all the junk you don't need, file the receipts you should keep, and put everything in its proper place. Flatten out your money and stack it so that all the bills face the right way. Clean out loose change and put it in a jar. (If you do this every day, you'll be amazed at how quickly it will pile up!)

• **Clean out the coat closet.** Take out all the things that don't belong in there and put them away properly. Hang up coats that have fallen or are slipping off hangers. Store scarves, hats, mittens, and earmuffs in a bin. Give away stuff that doesn't fit anymore or that nobody wants. Who knew you had all that space in there?

• **Balance your checkbook.** Quit griping or dreading it, and get it done.

• **Grab one stack on your desk.** Go through just one of the many stacks of things that need to be filed or put away, and clear it all out.

• **Dust your living room.** It should take only about five minutes to go over all of the flat surfaces, but it makes a perceptible difference.

• **Make your bed.** Don't make excuses about not having enough time when you get up in the morning. Just do it.

Go on a Reflection Walk

This strategy is good for people who (a) don't get enough exercise on most days and (b) tend to worry too much or mentally obsess about negative things in their lives. A reflection walk is a great, proactive way to take control simultaneously of your physical and mental state for one short, thirty-minute period. If you worry, sit at a desk, or feel rotten and scattered all day, then you need a daily reflection walk.

▦ ▦ ▦ ▦ ▪ **Clutter Control Quickie: Take a Fifteen-Minute Time-Out**

If clutter is stressing you out, set aside fifteen minutes to start, experience, and finish your own personal time. Go to a quiet room and instruct others you are not to be disturbed; then do something that you really want to do. Read, listen to music, sew, whittle, whistle, whatever. Just don't gyp yourself—be sure to do it for fifteen minutes solid! After you clear your brain, you'll be ready to continue with your day. ▪

A reflection walk can help relieve stress and make you feel better about yourself at the same time. Grab your most comfortable walking shoes, take a few deep breaths, and get ready to reflect on all the good things in your life. Walk for thirty minutes at a moderate pace—fast enough to feel as though you are getting a decent workout, but not so much that it wears you out, gets you frustrated, or makes your muscles sore. Think of the things you like about your job, the people you love, your favorite places to go and things to do, your kids, your pets—anything that makes you feel happy, positive, and energized. At first you might have to prod yourself to think like an active optimist, but eventually, subtly, it will take hold.

The challenge of the reflection walk is putting aside, for the full thirty minutes, all the stressful responsibilities, things that aren't working for you, and any other negativity that is holding you back or filling your life with unnecessary clutter. After the walk is over, these things might not seem so over-whelming once you've given yourself a little mental space and put them in perspective.

Seeing Green

Some people find that being in or even just looking at forests, mountains, flowers, and other natural beauty has a profound effect on how they feel about their lives, the world, and them-selves. Even if you live in the city, you can use nature to help you relieve stress and feel better. Surrounding yourself with beautiful images will give you little lifts all day long. Try some of these ideas:

• Add some scenery to your computer. Sign up on Webshots, at *www.webshots.com*, for free daily photos to use as computer wall-paper and screensavers. The site offers hundreds of beautiful images, including animals, unusual cloud formations, storms, and other natural phenomena. Maybe it's not as great as going on a vacation, but you'll probably look forward to picking out your new photo each morning, and it might help to revitalize your day.

• Instead of watching the usual lineup of sitcoms or dramas, watch the Discovery channel, Animal Planet, or any nature show on public television. It's good for your brain, food for your soul, and you just might learn something!

• Spend thirty minutes puttering around your own microenvironment. Even if your yard or the area around your apartment building is small, it probably contains some green stuff somewhere. Take your time as you meander, examining each tree, flower, and patch of grass. Don't think about anything else. Just see how much you can observe.

• Walk or drive to a park or a nicely landscaped neighborhood. Pay attention to everything, and fill up your brain with natural beauty. If you do, there won't be room for anxiety.

• Grow an herb garden or a small flower garden, either from seeds or by transplanting purchased plants into a large planter. Put the planter on your patio, deck, front step, or back step, or in a sunny window, then check and tend it daily.

• Go to your local library or bookstore and browse through a book that contains large color photographs of natural beauty. Let your imagination whisk you away for thirty minutes.

• Plan your next vacation around a natural wonder, such as the Grand Canyon, take a cruise to the Caribbean, camp in a national park or forest, or go to a beach in a neighboring town. Okay, this takes more than thirty minutes, but it's well worth it!

As pervasive as stress may be in all its forms, stress management techniques that really work are equally pervasive. You *can* manage, even eliminate, the negative stress in your life and help to get your body back to a more balanced state. All you have to do is find the stress management techniques that work best for you, and you'll be able to re-energize yourself and focus on regaining control of your life and your surroundings.

chapter 4

Stress-Proofing Your Life

WE'VE ALREADY SEEN THAT TOO MUCH STRESS can spark anything from an inability to concentrate, forgetfulness, restlessness, and fatigue, to irritability, excessive worrying, and even depression. How do you stress-proof your mind so that you no longer feel mentally cluttered, disorganized, and overloaded? Good stress management starts with tending to the basic essentials your body needs.

Getting Enough Sleep

If you aren't getting enough sleep, you are increasing your stress, compromising your health, and probably operating well below your potential. That's no way to control clutter. Getting enough sleep should be tops on your stress management to-do list.

Yet, according to the 2003 Omnibus Sleep in America Poll, conducted by the National Sleep Foundation *(www.sleep foundation.org)*, 27 percent of adults surveyed said that for at least a few days every month, they are so sleepy it interferes with their daily activities. In fact, 15 percent of adults experienced this level of daytime sleepiness at least a few days or more per week.

The average adult requires eight hours of sleep per night, and teenagers require 8.5 to 9.25 hours. Lack of sufficient sleep can make you feel irritable, depressed, and anxious. It can also decrease your ability to concentrate and understand information, cause you to be clumsier, react more slowly, make mistakes, or even have an accident.

When you get a good night's sleep, you'll find your stress management reserves growing. If you're having difficulty uncluttering your time to the point where you can't get in a good night's sleep, examine your schedule and the patterns that surround your sleeping routine. Then commit to changing it. Where are you wasting time during the day? How could you rearrange your schedule to get some things done in advance, allowing for an earlier bedtime? If you are staying up late to watch TV or surf the Internet, skip the media blitz for a few nights to see how extra sleep changes your mood and energy level.

▥ ▥ ▥ ▥ ▥ Clutter Control Quickie: Create a Bedtime Ritual

Parents are often advised to give their sleep-resistant children a routine, and this technique works for grownups, too. As you're getting ready for bed, do things that are conducive to relaxation—take a bath or shower; do a few minutes of deep breathing; sip a cup of herbal tea; read a good book instead of watching television; or write in your journal. Then, it's lights out. You'll soon find your bedtime ritual will greatly improve sleep time. ▥

When sleep eludes you, despite your best efforts, try these suggestions:

• Don't consume caffeine after lunch. Obviously, that includes coffee, tea, and soda, but don't forget, other common snacks, such as hot cocoa or chocolate, have caffeine as well. Certain over-the-counter pain and cold medications designed to keep you awake also contain caffeine, so read labels carefully.

• Stick to healthy, light, low-fat, low-carbohydrate dinners, because eating large dinners later at night can upset your digestive system. Fresh fruits and vegetables, whole grains (*not* refined), and low-fat protein like fish, chicken, beans, and tofu will put your body in a calmer, more balanced state for bedtime.

• If you need a snack at night, go for foods high in tryptophan, such as milk, turkey, peanut butter, rice, tuna, dates, figs, and yogurt, thirty to sixty minutes before bedtime. Tryptophan is an amino acid that encourages the body to produce serotonin, which helps you to sleep. Serotonin also regulates moods, helping you to feel good.

• Don't drink alcohol in the evening. Many people have a drink at night because they think it will help them sleep, but alcohol actually disrupts sleep patterns.

• Get enough exercise during the day, because it will help you to fall asleep faster and to sleep longer and more productively.

• Talk to your doctor if your sleep problems persist, because he or she might have another simple solution.

If it feels like you're wasting precious time by sleeping when you should be getting things done, keep reminding yourself that sleep *is* getting things done. While you sleep, your body is busy healing, recharging by conserving energy, growing and regenerating cells, and consolidating memory and discharging emotions through dreams. You're actually being very productive when you sleep, and you'll be even more productive during the day if you've had a good night's sleep.

Drinking More Water

If you're feeling anxious and stressed out, one of the best things you can do is drink a glass of water. Although the human body is about two-thirds water, many people are mildly dehydrated (3 percent to 5 percent below their body weight due to fluid loss) and don't realize it. Mild dehydration is more likely to occur after intense exercise, in extreme heat, while dieting, and after vomiting or diarrhea.

Without enough water, you're putting your body under stress, and you'll be less equipped to handle stress from other sources. Your body can't rally its energy in the cause of stress management because it is too busy trying to compensate for lack of water.

■ ■ ■ ■ Clutter Control Quickie: Just Breathe!

A few slow, deep breaths can stop a stress attack in its tracks and help you to center yourself again. Remember, with deep breathing, the *exhalation is the focus.* The easiest way to retrain yourself to breathe deeply is practicing while lying down. Breathe in through your nose, fill your torso from the bottom up, and breathe out through your mouth. Once you've mastered the feeling, try it sitting up. Measure your breathing with silent counting, making the exhalation twice as long as the inhalation. ▪

Ideally, you should drink sixty-four ounces, or eight cups, of water each day. That sounds like a lot, but if you space it throughout the day, it's not so much. To spruce plain water up a bit, try mineral-added bottled water, or add a wedge of lemon, lime, or orange. If you just have to have those bubbles, try club soda instead of caffeinated, sugar soda. Still not charmed? Dilute real fruit juice (not the sugar-added stuff) with half water or half club soda.

Taking Your Vitamins

Another way to build a healthy body ready to combat excessive stress is to make sure you aren't suffering from any basic deficiencies in vitamins, minerals, and phytochemicals (substances in plants thought to improve health and strengthen the immune system). While not everyone agrees that supplements are important, most of us don't get a chance to eat a completely balanced, well-rounded diet every single day. So, think of a supplement as extra insurance.

Among other things, the B vitamins, for instance, are thought to boost immunity, help metabolize food and produce energy, and reduce the effects of stress. Iron increases energy, and calcium is essential for lowering blood pressure, promoting sleep, and reducing symptoms of PMS—all of which can help to keep you feeling better and in a positive frame of mind, making it easier to control clutter. No matter how hectic your life gets, always make sure to eat a balanced diet, and take a multivitamin/multimineral tablet every day to strengthen your reserves and cover your nutritional bases.

Breaking Bad Habits

Everyone knows that drinking excessively, overeating, smoking, and other common vices can have a serious negative impact on health. But there are other bad habits that have more subtle effects on the quality of your life and your ability to get a handle on things. Maybe you're guilty of excessive overworking, and your work is impinging on your life—you have no personal time, you can never relax without thinking about work, and you have no privacy because people from work call you at home at all hours. Or maybe you've fallen prey to the media monster, and your free time revolves around digital cable, satellite dishes, premium movie channels, video rental stores, radio on the Internet, CD players in the car, high-speed Internet connections, DVD players . . . In this case, you're not alone, because the television is turned on in the average American home for seven hours and twelve minutes every day, and 66 percent of Americans eat dinner while watching TV. Just think about how much valuable time you're wasting!

■ ■ ■ ■ ■ Clutter Control Quickie: Cut Noise Clutter

If you always feel the need to hear the television, radio, or other background noise, whether you are paying attention or not, you've probably got a noise habit. Constant noise keeps your mind from focusing completely on anything and encourages fragmentation. Silence can be therapeutic and remarkably energizing. Carving out a space for some quiet stillness each day allows your body to recharge, so do it faithfully! ■

If these types of habits are taking up more than their fair share of your time and you are sacrificing other important priorities, then they're *bad* habits, and you need to reassess.

Seek balance in all of your habits and set boundaries, and you'll soon reduce your stress level, regain focus, and find time to start kicking your clutter for good!

Re-energizing with Exercise

According to an increasing number of experts, exercise might be the single most effective way to get stress under control, yet it's often the first thing to go when our schedules get too busy. Because there is no "deadline" associated with daily exercise, it's easy to bump it to the bottom of the priority list. Despite this inclination, find something you enjoy and stick to it. Expand your fitness horizons and keep an open mind. Regular exercise will help you clear your mind, relieve stress, and build more energy so that you're ready to tackle whatever needs tackling in your life.

If you take time away from the places and things in your life that need uncluttering, you just might find you have a whole new perspective when you go back to them. Here are some activities that can help you clear your mental clutter and soothe your stress levels.

Yoga

Because of its combination of specific postures, breathing exercises, and meditation, yoga is great for people who have a hard time slowing down (you'll learn how great it feels and how important it is to move your body with slow control) and for people who have a hard time engaging in high-impact, fast-paced exercise (yoga is adaptable to all fitness levels and it's decidedly low impact).

Yoga is among the more perfect stress management exercises. Its original purpose was to gain control over the body and bring it into a state of balance in order to free the mind for spiritual contemplation. Yoga can help you to master your body so that it doesn't master you.

Pilates

Pilates is a core-strengthening routine that uses either special machinery or a simple mat. Pilates concentrates on gaining control over the body's core, the torso, especially abdominal and back muscles. The exercises are part yoga, part gymnastics, and part ballet. Because Pilates has become so popular, classes and do-it-yourself Pilates books are widely available. Once learned from an expert, Pilates can easily be practiced at home on your own.

Tai Chi/Qigong

Tai chi and its precursor, Qigong, are ancient Chinese Taoist martial arts that have evolved to fit the twenty-first century. Rarely used today as methods of defense, tai chi consists of a series of slow, graceful movements in concert with the breath. It frees internal energy, keeps it flowing through the body, unites body and mind, and promotes good health and relaxation. Qigong involves specific movements and postures as well as other procedures such as massage and meditation to maintain and improve overall health and balance the body's internal energy.

The Great Outdoors

If you feel particularly inspired by great views, fresh air, and the smells of the natural world, choosing an outdoor exercise can inspire you to keep up with exercise. Whether you walk, jog, run, bicycle, roller blade, cross-country ski, hike, or climb mountains, exercising outdoors is good for your body and soul. Exercising outside can also help to keep you in touch with the natural world, which helps to put things in perspective.

Stress Relief for Your Mind and Spirit

Sometimes, in the quest to gain control of your life and your surroundings, "internal noise" is the biggest obstacle. When you feel stressed out beyond your usual limits, stress management techniques that help still, calm, and quiet the overactive mind are a must. These techniques are all about recognizing the thought processes and attitudes that increase stress and the tendency to cling to ideas that cause stress. Some of these are also related to physical stress management techniques, because the mind and body are inextricably connected. If you keep getting stuck in a clutter rut because of your own internal stresses, perhaps it's time to try meditation.

Meditation is particularly useful when it comes to clearing mental clutter, because it cuts through all our expectations and attitudes, and it helps to still the constant chatter in our heads so that we can think more clearly. It cultivates mental discipline and is exceptionally relaxing. Rather than letting our restless minds, worried thoughts, and anxious feelings get the better of us, meditation teaches us to still that mental ruckus, accept ourselves and our circumstances exactly as they are, and live peacefully in the present moment. That doesn't leave much room for stress.

▣ ▣ ▣ ▣ ▣ Clutter Control Quickie: The Power of Imagery

If you're feeling stressed, anxious, hopeless, or overwhelmed, take a mini vacation in your mind. Just close your eyes, relax, and breathe. Imagine wandering down a secluded tropical beach at sunset or cuddling in front of the fire in a cozy cabin in the woods. Wherever your mind takes you, the point is to escape by daydreaming a little. Consider it personal time to recharge. ▣

All types of meditation boil down to one thing: the honing of focus. Modern life promotes an unfocused mind. We get pulled in different directions at a constant, frantic pace as we are bombarded with stimuli from the media, from our environments, from people, from our computers. Work responsibilities and home life are full of so much to do that it isn't easy or even possible to spend much time on any one task, even if more time would result in higher quality. This get-it-done-fast-and-move-on way of life is hardly conducive to the concentration required for getting a handle on clutter!

Meditation puts a stop to the hectic craziness of everyday life. It allows your brain to hang up its "out to lunch" sign temporarily each time you practice. Those few minutes give your mind the opportunity to slow down, refocus, and rev up so that once again, you're ready to handle what needs to be done.

If you are interested in starting a meditation routine of your own, read through the different techniques below to get some ideas, then visit your local book store or surf the Internet for more information on the specifics of each type. Set aside a time each day—first thing in the morning, just before dinner, or just before bed are all good choices—and practice, practice, practice.

Zazen

Zazen is the sitting meditation of Zen Buddhism, but you don't need to practice Buddhism to benefit from zazen. All it requires is the ability to apply the seat of your pants to the floor and stay there for a while. It's hardly as easy as it sounds, though—especially when you're accustomed to accomplishing something at every moment of the day. Just sitting accomplishes something amazing when practiced daily. The mind becomes calmer, the muscles stay more relaxed, and suddenly you discover that *you* hold the reins, not your stress, not your overloaded schedule, not your cluttered home or office.

Walking Meditation

In Zen, walking meditation (kinhin) is the counterpart to sitting meditation (zazen), and it is exactly what it sounds like: meditation on the move. It's an excellent alternative or complement to sitting meditation. Some people like to sit for most of their meditation session and then spend the last few minutes in walking meditation. For others who practice sitting meditation for longer periods of time, walking meditation gets the body moving periodically without breaking the meditative flow. For people who just can't sit still, this can be a good way to ease into meditation without the commitment of sitting.

Yoga Meditation

Aside from its exercise benefits, yoga is also an ancient meditative tradition that was practiced in India for thousands of years, even before Hinduism arose. It might actually be the oldest of all meditation traditions. Most of the yoga practiced today is profoundly influenced by a text called the *Yoga Sutras,* which describes and explains yoga via a long list of aphorisms written thousands of years ago by a man named Patanjali. Many of these aphorisms can be seen as ancient and interesting approaches to stress management.

Shavasana

Shavasana, or the corpse pose, is actually a yoga asana, or exercise—one of those postures designed to help keep the body under control so that it doesn't interfere with the pursuit of meditation. Shavasana helps to rein in the body and get it working the way it is meant to work. For that very reason, shavasana is an excellent stress management technique.

Shavasana involves relaxing your body as you lie on your back, on the floor, with your arms flat and away from your body, your palms facing up, your legs about 2' apart, flat on the floor, and your feet falling to the side. This pose is an energizing way to start the day and a relaxing way to end it. Doing shavasana is like pushing the RESET button on your personal computer. It lets your body realign, re-energize, and reverse the insidious effects of stress.

Mindfulness Meditation

Mindfulness meditation is different than other meditations because it can be practiced anywhere, anytime, no matter what you are doing. It is simply focusing on total awareness of the present moment. Mindfulness meditation is inherent in many other forms of meditation but can also be practiced while walking, running, playing basketball, driving, studying, writing, reading, or eating. Anything you are doing can be done with mindfulness.

Mindfulness meditation has been popularized by both Easterners who have come West, such as Thich Nhat Hanh, the Vietnamese Buddhist monk, and Westerners such as Jon Kabat-Zinn, Ph.D., the founder and director of the Stress Reduction Clinic at the University of Massachusetts Medical Center. It is easy to do for short periods, but tough to maintain for an extended time, because our minds resist staying in the present moment.

Wherever you are, whatever you are doing, you can practice mindfulness meditation by consciously making the decision to be fully and completely aware of everything around you. Notice the impressions from all your senses. When your mind begins to think about something else, gently bring it back to the present moment. Don't judge the impressions of your senses. Just observe. The concentration and awareness that the practice brings might really come in handy when it's time to start tackling those cluttered closets and cramped kitchen cabinets!

Keeping Stress in Check

Fortifying your body with sleep, water, nutritional supplements, exercise, and mental relaxation will help to put you in good condition for managing stress. Learn how to unclutter your active mind, relax your tense muscles, and get rid of the long list of worries that keeps running through your head like a looped videotape. Mental stress and preoccupation can deter you from accomplishing the tasks at hand. When stress hits and your body begins to experience its effects, knowing how to react before they can do too much damage is a powerful skill. A healthy lifestyle is the best defense against stress and a great way to boost energy levels, maintain focus, and fuel motivation—all things that will aid you tremendously in your quest for clutter control.

chapter 5

Obstacles to Motivation and Organization

YOU CAN PLOT OUT YOUR SCHEDULE as efficiently as possible, clear your head of all its stress and distractions, and devise the most thorough clutter control plan imaginable, but if you can't get yourself motivated to tackle the disorganization in your life, you won't get anywhere. Motivation is what gets you going. It helps you through those seemingly impossible tasks and encourages you to stick with what you start. Lots of people believe motivation is derived only from outside forces. Often, however, personal inspiration—or lack thereof—has more to do with it.

Getting to the Root of the Problem

If you're feeling low on motivation, try to figure out why. When you cringe at the very thought of starting a clutter-control project, you know you've got a problem. Think about the things and feelings you associate with a particular task. Is it something that you had a tough or unpleasant time with in the past? Are you unsure about your ability to complete the task properly or afraid that the outcome won't be good? Was the project forced on you, so you have negative feelings about it from the get-go? Maybe you're just too tired to put forth the effort it will take, or you're really busy and you know the project will consume a huge chunk of your time.

Whatever the root of your lack of motivation, the best way to dispel those negative associations is simply to jump in and get started. You're probably thinking it sounds a bit counterintuitive to begin a project without any sort of enthusiasm—or notion of how, exactly, you're going to get it done. But even if you feel like you don't know what you're doing, just doing something that pertains to the task will usually serve as a good initial motivator.

■ ■ ■ ■ ■ **Clutter Control Quickie: Energy Boosts**

When you're tired, you're probably not inspired to accomplish a lot. If this is your problem, grab a healthy snack. Getting some food into your system will up your energy level. Or, take a power nap. A quick snooze will help you shake that sleepy feeling and give you a fresh outlook on the job at hand. You can even do some exercises to stretch your muscles, accelerate your heart rate, and get your blood—and creative juices—flowing. ■

If you're feeling stressed or overwhelmed by the prospect of completing an *entire* job, remember to break it down into smaller steps. Let's say, for instance, you just can't muster the motivation to clean up that huge pile of dishes in your sink. Don't sit there and stew about how many dishes there are to wash or how long it will take you. Just get up off the couch. Don't think about it; do it. Once you're standing, it will be easier to head toward the kitchen. Chances are, once you wash that first dish and see that even the tiniest bit of progress has been made, you'll want to keep going.

Outsmarting Sensory Overload

Sometimes, when there's so much clutter around you, your senses become overwhelmed with the amount of work staring you in the face. If you're stuck in sensory overload, the size of your projects might be a huge stumbling block. A big project, regardless of importance, can be intimidating. Once intimidation takes hold, there's no stopping the number of obstacles that will suddenly materialize.

Take procrastination, for instance. When faced with a giant project looming in the distance, most people linger behind as long as possible and put off that necessary confrontation. They know in the back of their minds that the task will only be harder to complete if they wait until the last minute, yet the fear of tackling it paralyzes their courage and reasoning abilities.

Maybe you don't procrastinate, and instead, when faced with an overwhelming project, you jump right in and work non-stop. You've already seen what happens when you dive in without designing a plan. Without a strategy, a big project swallows you whole. You need your plan of attack, so don't skip the schedule organization stage.

When feeling overloaded, the first thing to do is know your deadline. It might already have been set by a higher authority, or you might have to set it yourself. If the latter is the case, take your time analyzing how much work it will take to complete the task correctly. Be realistic in the time span you give yourself. Create a clear picture of the completed project in your mind, contemplate any possible problems or obstacles that might unexpectedly arise, and prepare a counterattack.

By breaking big tasks into smaller sections, your apprehension will begin to fade. It won't seem so overwhelming if you shift focus from the size of the task to the size of the individual steps. This way, you'll build your confidence, and the determination to complete the task will set in.

Taking Breaks

If you're suffering from sensory overload, you need to learn the value of a break. You might believe that it's better to plow through a project so you don't interrupt momentum but, inevitably, your mind will get tired, you'll get stuck, and it will be hard to accomplish anything. This is the point where your disappointment builds and you start to feel like a failure. You probably blame yourself for not working hard enough, not being able to stick to your project, cracking under too much stress, or not giving yourself enough time to get things done, when in reality, a quick break might have made all the difference.

Taking a break doesn't interrupt momentum. It gives you a chance to clear your head, think about what you want to accomplish next, and renew your energy and direction. This way, you're ready for action when you resume your project.

▨ ▨ ▨ ▨ ▨ Clutter Control Quickie: Trick Yourself

When you have a big task to accomplish, breaking it down into a series of smaller tasks is essential for staying focused. Just don't consider the steps to be steps. Instead, think of them as individual projects. This way, you'll divert your focus from the big task and set your mind at ease. ▨

Breaks don't always have to be a set length, nor do they require you to leave your work area. They're simply changes; and change is good. Just don't make your breaks so long that you lose touch with what you are working on. And don't spend as much time breaking as you do working! Short, frequent breaks with a couple of extended breaks thrown in work best when you're trying to accomplish a big task. Remember, the primary goal is to keep your body and mind fresh and focused.

Keeping Emotions in Check

Your own emotions can be a big enemy—or asset—when it comes to clutter control. Think about what you did the last time you were sad. Maybe you moped around the house, called in sick to work, or went shopping to cheer yourself up. But you probably did not reorganize your kids' bedrooms. Or maybe you did. In that case, you might be one of the lucky ones who recognizes the value of exerting a little control over your surroundings when the going gets tough.

There are so many things that can spin out of control over the course of an average day—you get stuck in traffic, everything goes wrong at work, the bank messes up and forgets to process that deposit you just made last week. It's enough to send your emotions over the edge. But no matter how annoyed, frustrated, angry, or whatever else you are, you can always come home and improve your surroundings. Okay, maybe cleaning up the bathroom isn't the first thing that comes to mind when you're feeling horrible after a bad day, but sometimes the immediate, concrete results you see when you clean or reorganize can be just what the doctor ordered!

■ ■ ■ ■ ■ Clutter Control Quickie: Put Emotions to Good Use

The next time you're so angry that you're ready to pounce on the next person who looks at you cross-eyed, channel all of that energy into tackling a necessary task. Taking your anger out on a project—instead of a person—will effectively release tension and also allow you to use your time more wisely. ■

Emotions have tremendous impact on everything you do, so take them into consideration when embarking on your clutter-control missions. This isn't to say that you are always able to gauge your emotions days in advance. But if you consider what your feelings and reactions toward a particular activity will be, your efforts will be more productive.

Emotions only take a toll on your productivity when you give them control. You can't always control how you feel, but you do have some control over your reactions to your emotions. Say, for instance, you are easily angered and frustrated, and every little thing that goes wrong gets under your skin. You can either obsess about the things that make you angry and blow up at everyone who crosses your path, or you can keep those feelings in check and stay focused on the tasks at hand. This isn't to say you should bury all your feelings deep inside—that's just asking for trouble. But you can use reason and willpower to overcome your emotions so that they don't thwart your actions.

Beware of Parkinson's Law

We all know about Murphy's Law—and if your clutter control endeavors have amounted to nothing more than a comedy of errors thus far, you probably feel as if it directly applies to you. But there's another, lesser-known law that might be at work. According to *Parkinson's Law*, the book by C. Northgate Parkinson, work expands to fill the time allotted for it. The author's description of bureaucracy and human folly, while geared toward government offices and other large organizations, might apply to your own activities as well. For instance, if you give yourself an hour to clean up the yard, it will take you an hour. But if you spread your yard work out over four hours, you will accomplish the same amount of work in that longer period of time.

Parkinson's Law can cause you to place greater importance on activities that have little value. Understand this concept and see if it applies in your current use of time. This recognition might not solve all of your problems, but it might help you to make better use of time so that you can conquer clutter more effectively. One caveat: If you realize you can do the same amount of work in half the time, you might procrastinate until a deadline looms large. So just make sure you never cut things too close.

Excuses, Excuses

Everyone makes excuses from time to time, but for some, excuses are the rule rather than the exception. Constantly making excuses is a hard habit to break, especially if it's something learned in childhood. If you know you're not accomplishing everything you could or should, think hard about all the excuses you make each day, and notice the time and energy you waste on this nasty little habit.

It's relatively easy to recognize the repercussions of making excuses to other people—for starters, you probably feel guilty about it, and the people you affect with your excuses most likely feel hurt and let down, too. But what happens when you make excuses to yourself? This is when you really start wasting your time and energy.

Let's say you have this big plan to clean out your attic next Saturday. This isn't exactly the ideal way to spend a day off, but you know it needs to be done. So you anticipate and plan for all the proper steps—you carve out sufficient time from your schedule, then you buy cleaning supplies, super-sized garbage bags, plastic storage bins, shelves, and all sorts of paraphernalia to help you clear out and reorganize. Now, when Saturday morning rolls around you have nothing left to do but get to it.

■ ■ ■ ■ ■ Clutter Control Quickie: Eliminate Excuses

If you can't seem to get anything done because you're always busy making excuses, start keeping track of each one you use. Write your excuses down, if you have to, then don't allow yourself to repeat any of them. Eventually, you'll get tired of inventing new ones, and you'll have to focus on the tasks at hand. ■

You jump out of bed bright and early, but when you peer through the blinds you see it's a gorgeous, sunny day. All of a sudden, excuses galore pop into your head, telling you that it would be better to postpone the project. After all, it makes more sense to save an indoor project for a rainy day. And you really could use the fresh air and exercise. Now you're stuck fighting with yourself, because you know you should get the job done. Then the decision-making process comes into play, as you weigh the pros and cons of each choice. What have you accomplished by concocting all of these excuses? A whole lot of nothing. But you've probably wasted a whole lot of time in the process. Stop wasting time playing these games with yourself, and start your project anyway. If you got going right away, you'd get the job done quickly and efficiently. That way, maybe you'd even have time to spare, to enjoy that great weather at the end of the day.

Adjusting Your Attitude

If you're the glass-is-half-empty type who only sees the downside of things, it can have a huge impact on your ability to conquer your clutter! You'll never be able to put things in the proper order—your home, your time, or even your brain—if you feel defeated by a daunting task before you even start it. Being negative is a habit, and you can stop it right now. First, become aware of when you tend to be negative by keeping a negativity journal. Then, whenever you feel like being negative, don't express it out loud, write it down instead. Once you get it out of your system on the page, you can look at it more objectively later; eventually, you'll start to see patterns and catch yourself in the act.

The more you get used to halting your negative reactions and replacing them with neutral or positive reactions, the less you'll find yourself reacting negatively. And you can bet you'll feel a lot more energetic and motivated if you approach your clutter control efforts with a positive attitude!

Optimism Therapy

So, you think you are a confirmed pessimist? Don't knock optimism before you try it—looking at the world through rose-colored glasses has its benefits. Often, optimists are actually happier and healthier because they feel as if they have control over their lives, whereas pessimists are more likely to believe that life controls them.

Psychologists determine whether people have optimistic or pessimistic characters based on their explanatory style when describing an unfortunate event. The explanatory style has three parts:

1. *The internal/external explanation:* Optimists tend to believe that external factors cause misfortune; pessimists tend to blame themselves (the internal factor).
2. *The stable/unstable explanation:* Optimists tend to see misfortune as unstable or temporary; pessimists tend to see misfortune as stable or permanent.
3. *The global/specific explanation:* Optimists tend to see

problems as specific to a situation; pessimists tend to see problems as global—that is, unavoidable and pervasive.

Because of their tendencies, pessimists might feel like they are under more stress than optimists, even though in reality both are under the same amount of stress. Optimists are also more likely to engage in positive, proactive behaviors, such as exercising and eating well. Pessimists, on the other hand, sometimes adopt a fatalistic attitude, thinking that since what they do doesn't matter anyway, they might as well do whatever is easiest. If you're a pessimist who has problems with clutter control, you can probably hear yourself making excuses right now. You might be thinking, "What good will it do if I clean up the kitchen, because the kids will just mess it all up again five minutes later," or "My closets are way too tiny to fit all the junk that I have—I'll never be able to organize them."

If this sounds familiar, it's time to engage in a little optimism therapy. Pretending to be an optimist can actually make you feel like one and can help your body learn to respond like an optimist, too.

At the beginning of each day, before you even have time to get too pessimistic, tell yourself that no matter what happens, it will still be a good day. Remind yourself that *you* choose to make your day good or bad. Remember, it's all about attitude. Choose one area or part of your day and vow to be an optimist in that area. During that period, every time you begin to think negatively or say something pessimistic, immediately replace it with something optimistic. It might seem weird at first, but soon you'll see that your attitude will change. Eventually, you'll feel as if you have the power to take control of things around you and you'll start to reshape your life and your surroundings to better suit your needs. Soon, all of that clutter control won't seem like such a daunting, insurmountable task!

When Procrastination Rears Its Ugly Head

Okay, here comes the big one. One of the toughest obstacles to motivation—the "P" word. Procrastinators are highly skilled individuals, and most clutter bugs are no exception. After all, you wouldn't be so inundated with all this stuff if you'd grabbed the bull by the horns and gotten rid of it in the first place. Procrastination requires the ability to create convincing excuses— convincing enough to persuade not only others but yourself as well. A procrastinating pack rat concocts all sorts of creative reasons to hold on to—and refuse to part with—all sorts of stuff. You just can't bear to part with those scraps of wrapping paper because they remind you of your birthday, right? If this sounds like you, give yourself a pat on the back for being so creative, then pour all of that creativity into actually accomplishing something. Devise some equally innovative ways to control your clutter.

Procrastination is simply the postponement of an activity that could—and most times should—be done sooner rather than later. It can also be Personal Enemy Number One when it comes to overcoming clutter. Don't get down on yourself about it, though. Everyone procrastinates sometimes. It's only a problem when procrastination becomes a way of life. Regardless of your degree of dawdling, the results are ultimately the same—an increase in stress, a decrease in self-esteem, a job hastily finished (or sometimes not finished at all), guilty feelings, and, of course, the loss of valuable time.

▨ ▨ ▨ ▨ ▪ Clutter Control Quickie: Progress Reports

If you find yourself procrastinating or having trouble staying on track with your clutter control projects, keep a log of your progress. It might sound strange, but a weekly or monthly progress report can help you to remain motivated and focused as you work toward accomplishing a big project or a series of smaller tasks. ▪

The most obvious reason for procrastination is simply not wanting to do work that needs to be done. Look at the big picture, though. Sure, you aren't going to enjoy the activity while it lasts, but once it's over, you'll get to wipe it off of your list, and you'll feel a huge sense of accomplishment.

Let's say you absolutely detest doing laundry. You know it needs to be done, but you can survive for a few more days. So you put it off, even though you have the time to do it. Instead, you make phone calls, lounge on the couch, and generally waste time. Now you've procrastinated the task at hand, and you haven't filled the time with anything more productive. You might think you're having more fun by not doing your laundry, but the task undone will gnaw at the back of your mind, putting a damper on more pleasant activities. Not to mention the fact that the laundry pile continues to grow, which only creates more work. In the end, you'll be forced to spend more time doing a chore you hate. If you had just tackled the laundry when it needed to be done, you could have cleared the thought from your mind and then enjoyed your time doing other things.

Fear Factor

Fear of failure plays a big role in procrastination. Each of us has struggled with this; fear is a normal human reaction. Many people advertently or inadvertently use the fear of failure to postpone or deny activities or actions that could better their lives, if given the chance. The fear overrides the possibilities.

Let's say you've been assigned the task of spearheading a big project at work. There are many elements involved, and you might even be directing the workload of others as you juggle your own. This requires uncluttering your schedule, making adequate time to do the work, and coordinating and organizing with everyone else involved. But maybe you're afraid you're not up to the challenge, and because of your fear of failure, you have put off handling the project, to the point where you might not even be able to accomplish it properly. You'll miss a great opportunity to show your capabilities if you allow your fears to override your best interests. In some instances, you might actually prompt a self-fulfilling prophesy, because you could lose control over the situation you fear.

The flip side of this coin is a fear of success and, believe it or not, this is common as well. Everyone wants to succeed at the things they set out to accomplish in life, but what happens when you reach an ideal peak? Maybe you're afraid that once your house is shipshape, you won't be able to maintain it. Or maybe you think as soon as you turn your clutter around, you'll be expected to keep everything perfect. Can you take that pressure, or will it be too much to handle?

Most often low self-esteem is the primary issue to be dealt with here. Fearing success usually means that you are unsure of your ability. If you put your fear aside and think about things rationally, however, you'll see that if you are capable of the effort and skill it took to accomplish what needs to be done, you've already made it past the most difficult stages, and you can surely handle the maintenance that comes later.

Whatever the cause of your procrastination, you're going to have to get past it if you want to unclutter your life. Here are some tips to help you:

• **Realize what has been holding you back.** Make a list of activities and chores you have been putting off, analyze the list, and figure out what's causing you to postpone each task. When you discover and face the reason behind your procrastination, it will be easier to surmount.

• **Accept responsibility.** Decide whether an activity needs to be done and whether it is you who needs to do it. If you take on the chore, accept responsibility for its completion. Reap the rewards if it is completed, but be prepared for the consequences if it's not.

• **Reorder your to-do list.** Move the jobs you dislike the most to the top of your list. If you can look forward to moving down to the other, more enjoyable tasks, you'll accomplish more. Writing down the benefits of completing each task is also good for a little added motivation.

• **Don't feed your self-defeating attitudes.** Getting down on yourself only wastes time and prevents you from accomplishing things.

• **Ditch the creative excuses.** As soon as your attention to the task at hand is distracted by an excuse, challenge the excuse with reason.

Reward Yourself

Rewards work great in the battle against procrastination. Rewarding yourself for a job well done boosts self-esteem and motivates you to complete future tasks. If you've ever trained a dog, you probably know about positive reinforcement training, which most instructors use today. People also respond to positive reinforcement. Dogs—and humans—do things for two main reasons: either to benefit and be rewarded or to avoid something negative. Obviously, benefiting from a reward is far more compelling. Think of it in terms of your anticlutter crusade. You *know* that you should clean up your clutter because you don't want to live in a pig sty (the negative consequence you should be avoiding), yet it's still really easy to put off the cleanup.

If you frame changes you are trying to make in terms of positive reinforcement, you are much more likely to be successful. You probably don't do backflips for dog biscuits, but that doesn't mean you don't like treats. Make a list of your personal "people treats," and every time you've got some tough clutter to conquer, choose a treat as an incentive for accomplishing the task. Promise yourself that once you get the job done, you can order in or go out to dinner instead of cooking;

get a massage; go to a yoga class; rent that new movie on DVD you've been dying to see; call a friend for a catch-up chat. Use anything that will get you going. These rewards will keep you thinking positive, feeling relaxed, and enjoying the process of cleaning up and clearing out.

Just be sure to keep the following guidelines in mind when planning rewards:

1. The reward cannot exceed the activity. If you're faced with the dreaded task of cleaning out your refrigerator, for example, you cannot reward yourself with a trip to Hawaii.
2. The activity cannot exceed the reward. If it's spring-cleaning time, and you take apart the entire house from top to bottom (garage included), one bite of ice cream does not serve as an appropriate incentive.
3. A reward cannot conflict with a to-do. In other words, you cannot reward yourself by procrastinating or eliminating an item on your to-do list.
4. A reward cannot conflict with any goals or priorities you have set. For instance, if your goal is to reduce clutter from under your bed, you can't clear everything out and then just stick it somewhere else. You really do need to organize things!
5. You cannot stockpile rewards because they will lose their individual meaning if grouped with others. A reward does not work as a reward if it does not reflect upon the task completed.

The Pains of Perfectionism

Perfectionism can be just as bad as procrastination. In some instances, perfectionism can even be a catalyst for procrastination. Take, for example, a perfectionist who needs to clean out a junk drawer. He knows the job has to get done, but he won't even begin to do it until he finds the *perfect* organizer to fit nicely within the drawer. Or perhaps he thinks he just doesn't have the time to sit down and go through each and every scrap of paper to determine its worth. Whatever the reasoning, he believes if he can't do the job well, then it just won't be done at all.

Perfectionism hinders your ability to produce results. In the mind of a perfectionist, success is achieved only through perfection. Anything short of perfection is simply unacceptable. But realistically, perfection does not exist and, therefore, the perfectionist never attains success.

■ ■ ■ ■ ■ Clutter Control Quickie: Space out Your Time Slots

If you're a perfectionistic overachiever who oversaturates your day with too many activities, start using a calendar that breaks the day down into bigger time slots, such as hours instead of fifteen-minute blocks. This will help you to set more reasonable goals and discourage you from overloading your day. ■

Perfectionists view all mistakes as failures, and they often take an "all or nothing" approach toward things. This hampers productivity, because if unrealistic goals are set, inevitably they cannot be met, and this creates a sense of failure. That failure brings about low self-esteem and an even greater compulsion to get it perfect the next time. Thus, a vicious cycle is created.

Striving to get something accomplished perfectly is an admirable goal, as long as you equate perfect with your best efforts and realize that perfection in itself does not exist. If you are a perfectionist, you set extremely high standards of achievement for yourself. Use that motivation to your benefit, by setting your goals at a challenging, but healthy level, and you'll accomplish a lot.

Remember that you are human, and mistakes are tools for learning. Pay attention to them, but don't dwell on them or regard them as failures. Don't pick every little thing you do to pieces, and try to look at the positive side of what you're accomplishing rather than scrutinizing the flaws in your progress. Don't let your perfectionism stand in the way of getting a job done. Jump right into things, and then recognize what you *do* accomplish, not what you don't.

chapter 6

Clutter Control Basics

ORGANIZATION. SIMPLIFICATION. Elimination. Relaxation. If you're in the throes of clutter catastrophe, all these "-ation" words probably sound like pipe dreams, right? Don't worry, organization *is* attainable; you just have to learn to live more simply by eliminating what isn't necessary. Reducing clutter reduces stress, and reducing stress will help you to foster a peaceful, relaxed lifestyle and living environment.

Right now, you might think that organization is way out of your league. You have no idea where to start, and you probably wouldn't know where to go once you did. Let's get one thing straight: Organization isn't some secret, elusive solution, it's right within your reach. All it takes is a system—any system—that works for you. If you can come up with systems that allow you to weed out what you don't need, locate items quickly and easily, keep track of everything, and live and work efficiently and effectively, then you're on your way. Clutter control is a personal thing. The ultimate goal is to simplify your life, and that is not an idea you can just borrow.

■ ■ ■ ■ ■ Clutter Control Quickie: Remote Control Retrieval

If your TV remote control often gets lost, it's a good idea to assign it a spot within arm's reach of the couch. Designate an end table nearby, or maybe even consider hanging a pouch container off the side of the couch. Then, when you are done with the remote, put it back in its place so you'll automatically know where to reach for it next time. ■

Don't be overwhelmed by the prospect of starting your clutter control mission. Take a look at everything around you and decide if you have any systems that are currently working. If so, it's a great idea to expand on these since they came about naturally and probably make intuitive sense to you. Don't overlook the simple things. Even something as simple as hanging up a wet towel every day in a particular spot is its own system. Use your pre-existing systems to spiral outward. Start small with other household items, and then see if your systems can be applied to other areas of your life.

Evaluating Your Living Space

Now that you've focused yourself mentally, turn that new energy outward to tackle the spatial disorganization around you. But before you develop a full-blown plan to reorganize your living space, spend a few minutes evaluating it as it is right now.

1. What do you like the most about your current living space?
2. How would you rate the cleanliness of your living space?
   - ❑ Disgustingly dirty and unsanitary
   - ❑ Totally disorganized and filled with clutter
   - ❑ Sanitary and comfortable, but needs improvement
   - ❑ Totally organized, highly functional, and comfortable
3. In terms of physical space, how would you rate your home currently? (Check all that apply.)
   - ❑ Way too small and cluttered
   - ❑ A decent size, but cluttered
   - ❑ Just the right size for my needs
   - ❑ In need of an overhaul
   - ❑ Lacking storage space
   - ❑ Too dirty
   - ❑ Highly impractical and uncomfortable
   - ❑ Outdated
   - ❑ Too large
4. What do you like the least about your living space?
5. What improvements would you like to make to your home? Do certain areas need to be repaired, updated, renovated, or remodeled?

6. Based on the physical space available in your home, does your furniture and décor give you maximum functionality and comfort? How could you better use your space?

7. What are your living habits in each room of your home? (Consider other members of your household as well.) Create a list of your primary activities in each area. For example, in addition to cooking and eating, do you use your kitchen for paying bills, working on the computer, or talking on the telephone? Consider primary areas, such as living room, dining room, bedrooms and bathrooms, but also remember to think about closets, laundry room, basement, attic, garage, or other storage spots.

8. As you walk through your home, pinpoint the areas that contain the most disorganization and clutter. What types of clutter are you dealing with in each area? On a scale of one to five, with five being the most disorganized and clutter-filled, rate each room.

9. Next, determine the cause of your clutter. What are the three biggest problems with each room? Think in terms of design, layout, functionality, space limitations, and so on. Is there simply too much stuff in the room? Does your furniture layout limit the room's functionality? Is the room short on storage? Could existing storage space be used better? Have you just been too lazy to do anything about your clutter?

10. Finally, take a few minutes to consider everything you could do to create a more ideal living environment. Can you reorganize or put things into storage, or is it time to donate or discard stuff you really don't want or need? This list can include anything from major tasks, like completely renovating the kitchen, to smaller jobs, like finding a better system for dealing with all of the books stacked on your living room floor.

Now that you recognize problem areas, consider what you can do to stop generating clutter in your home. Keep a running list of tasks you can start immediately to curb your clutter and create a more enjoyable living space.

Breaking Organization into Manageable Tasks

Remember that with any large or daunting project, getting started is often the hardest part. Trying to accomplish too much at once is overwhelming and frustrating. Instead of preparing to overhaul your entire home immediately, divide the work into a series of smaller, more achievable tasks. Start by taking inventory of the clutter around you: Break your home down into small areas that you can tackle one by one, in a few hours or a day.

Suppose, for instance, you decide that your bedroom is the biggest disaster in your home, and that's the perfect place to start. You might be in the habit of putting dirty clothes on the floor instead of in the laundry hamper. Maybe you need to go to the dry cleaner more frequently, or you need to start putting your shoes on a shoe rack in the closet instead of leaving them scattered on the bedroom floor. You might need storage shelves or a more efficient dresser.

▪ ▪ ▪ ▪ ▪ **Clutter Control Quickie: The One-Year Rule**

As you're clearing your clutter, most of the time it will be easy to know if an item is worth keeping or not. Occasionally, though, you might be unsure about parting with something. When this happens, pack the item up and store it in your attic or basement temporarily. Then, if you don't miss it after a year, you can be sure it's time to toss it! ▪

After you decide on an area and think about why it is so cluttered, list the specific organizational steps you need to take, such as buying shelves and a shoe rack, discarding all those clothes you haven't worn in a year, and so on. Also create a deadline for completing the project, decide on a budget, and list any tools or other items you need to purchase or borrow to complete the job. Finally, consider whether you need assistance from an organizational expert, electrician, plumber, contractor, architect, or some other outside professional.

Sorting Through Your Stuff

If you really want to unclutter your life, start sorting. All that stuff you own takes up your space, time, and energy. Whether you keep meaning to repair a zipper on those pants you rarely wear, or you're continuously tripping over that doll your daughter doesn't even play with, stuff gets in your way. This hardly means you should ditch all the comforts of home and live on the streets. Just take stock of what you own and how it might or might not be cluttering up your life.

The following sections identify some of the main problems that need to be addressed when first attempting to conquer the clutter around you. They are by no means the only obstacles you'll have to tackle, but if you keep these things in mind, you'll get off to a good start.

Find a Home for Everything

Does it feel as if your keys grow legs and run away from you every morning? Are you constantly tripping over shoes, sporting equipment, and all sorts of other things because they're strewn all over the house? Does your assistant complain that he or she can't find *anything* in your office? If so, you need to find a home for all of your stuff!

It's pretty basic when you think about it, but it's hard to follow through when you're always getting sidetracked by other things that take up your attention. Think about all those things that you're always losing—and then frantically searching for. Items you use every day deserve their own space. Get into a routine of placing items in their homes, and stick to it.

Dozens of household and office items can be given their own homes. Utensils, phone numbers, addresses, books, hair accessories, medication, jewelry—you name it, and there's sure to be a place just waiting for it. If everything remains scattered in a cluttered mess around your home or office, you're wasting valuable time—not to mention driving yourself nuts. Once you give things a home, those items that evade you will be under your control.

▪ ▪ ▪ ▪ ▪ Clutter Control Quickie: Set Realistic Goals

If you suddenly decide you want to overhaul your entire house from top to bottom in one weekend, you're probably setting yourself up for deflated expectations—not to mention a whole lot of stress. But if you begin by focusing on one room or area, you'll be much more likely to meet your goal in a finite period of time. Incorporate these tasks into your to-do list and determine approximately how long each task will take. ▪

Finding a home for things doesn't necessarily mean that all your stuff needs to be tucked away and hidden from view. It simply involves knowing exactly where to look for particular items. If you've already thought of this and have homes for certain items, but they just don't seem to work, you've probably overlooked a glitch in your system. Maybe not everyone in the house is aware of where things go, so they keep getting misplaced. Or perhaps the layout goes against your natural instincts. If you've carved out a space in your bedroom for umbrellas but you don't think about whether or not it's raining until you hit the door, chances are the umbrellas are going to find themselves a new home on your foyer floor. Look for these kinds of glitches in your clutter control system, and adapt your plan accordingly.

Organize Your Bills

Most people have lots of bills that pile up every month and you just push them aside until it's time to pay them, then toss the remains out of sight. If this sounds like you, you need to set up an organizational system. Designate a specific place to put your bills as soon as you receive them. Something as simple as a folder will work. Before placing the bills in the folder, open them, and write the date they are due on the outside of the envelope. Place a stamp and your return address (use labels if you have them ready-made) on the return envelope. Then, schedule two separate days a month to pay your bills. When it comes time to pull out the checkbook, you will have everything you need right there. Also consider setting up direct deduction payment schedules, if the service is available.

■ ■ ■ ■ ■ Clutter Control Quickie: Group Similar Items

Keep things you need to accomplish a certain task, such as receipts and bills, in one place. Better yet, keep a pen, stamps, and return address labels in the same area as your bills. Paid bill stubs and receipts should have a designated storage space. You might choose a filing cabinet, an organizer made specifically for paying bills, or a basic paper tray. Use whatever you think will work, just make sure to use it faithfully. ■

If you want to be extremely organized, keep a filing system. Give each monthly bill its own folder and keep all correspondence and receipts there for future referral. Also write the check number on the copy of the bill you keep for your records. This will allow you easy access to payment information should the need arise. And you'll be able to recall quickly if a bill has been paid.

The Paper Chase

If you're having a hard time knowing where to start with sorting through your stuff, try separating all of the paper out first. This is guaranteed to cut through a huge chunk of clutter. For starters, go through all of the random pieces of paper piling up all over your house. If the print is too faded to read, it automatically goes—no ifs, ands, or buts. Newspapers, magazines, newsletters, and anything dated prior to the previous month all go, too. Rifle through everything dated within the previous or current month, and see if there's anything worth keeping or reading. If so, clip what you want, and throw out the rest of the bulk.

Most likely, there will be some papers you feel you should keep, for financial purposes, sentimental reasons, or whatever else. Use good judgment here—no one's telling you you should throw away the first love letters your husband ever wrote you just because they're old. But if you're holding onto something more trivial, something you won't even glance at again until the next time you decide to go into an organizing frenzy, then you need to chuck it! Once you figure out the paper puzzle, you'll feel much better about tackling the rest of your clutter.

Limit Your Lists

How many lists do you write in the course of a year? Think about all those grocery lists, mailing lists, Christmas lists, people-to-thank lists, books-to-read lists, movies-to-watch lists, home-improvements lists, wish lists, and so on. There's nothing wrong with creating lists. In fact, they're necessary at times. You need to have a list of priorities, a to-do list, and a list of goals, to name a few. But when you create lists that have very little value, confuse you, make your life more complicated, or waste your time, you've reached a point of diminishing returns. An overabundance of poorly sorted, unnecessary lists can really trip you up—especially if you spend so much time rifling through just to find one thing you're looking for. All these lists can make you feel rushed, heighten feelings of pressure, and prompt irrelevant anxiety. You might even lose sight of what is important amid all the itemized papers.

Don't start lots of different, partial lists in various places throughout the day; try to keep just a few master lists. Use lists to help you remember, to plan ahead, and to keep your priorities in line, so that your life will be easier and more organized. Take a look at the lists you have now. Are there any things that could be combined? For instance, if making a phone call is on your to-do list for today, write the phone number of the person you are calling on that same list. This way, you'll have the information you need in front of you and won't waste time searching.

■ ■ ■ ■ Clutter Control Quickie: Keep Trash Bags on Hand

Before you start clearing out, grab some trash bags or large boxes. Empty closets, cabinets, drawers, and shelves, and place the contents into piles: one for items you need to keep handy, one for things you can keep in storage, one for stuff you want to sell or give away, and one for junk you need to throw out. ■

The Moving Mess

Moving is a huge headache, but it's one that we all must endure periodically. There are ways to make it more organized, time-efficient, and less painstaking. Even if you aren't planning on moving anytime soon, read this section and keep the information in the back of your mind, because it will come in handy sooner or later. Remember, you don't want to move into a new place, only to find yourself in a bigger jumble of clutter than the one you packed up at your last place.

There are several things to consider when organizing a move. For instance, how far are you moving from your current location? How much stuff do you have to move? Do you have enough people lined up to help you? Can you take any time off from work to make your move? Be sure to take your time with this and consider all the factors.

In order to be efficient about your move, you need to plan carefully and be realistic about the amount of time it will take to organize, sort, pack, label, transport, unload, unpack, and then redistribute everything properly in your new home. That's a lot of work. It shouldn't be a rush job, so give yourself a space cushion when scheduling each step of the process.

Following are some suggestions to help you cut the chaos and clutter involved in moving, to make the process flow smoothly and efficiently:

• **Create a to-do list.** That's right, you have to-do lists for everything else, and this is no exception. Pull in the rest of your family to brainstorm. You'll be able to figure out a workable schedule from this to-do list.

• **Get rid of what you don't need.** Consider everything you own, and do some serious eliminating. If you don't need something, donate it, sell it, or flat out scrap it. Whatever you get rid of now will save you time in the long run, because it's that much less for you to pack, move, unpack, and reorganize in your new place.

• **Take inventory of those items that are left.** If you are hiring a moving company, separate the inventory into two categories: things the moving company is going to handle and things you are taking with you.

• **Stay room-oriented when you pack.** Pack items that belong together in the same box. Don't pack your son's clothes with your daughter's clothes, even though it may be easier to pull them all out of the dryer and put them straight into a box. It takes more time to pack this way, but you'll avoid an all-out disaster when you're unpacking if you keep things organized.

• **Don't label boxes with generic names; give them numbers.** Each time you pack a box, give that box a number, place that number at the top of an index card, and write all the items in the box on that card. This way, when you desperately need an item already packed (and this almost always happens), all you have to do is locate the item on the index card and find the corresponding box.

• **Unload boxes and furniture in their appropriate rooms.** When you haul everything into your new place, don't dump it all together, out in the open. All of that clutter will stress you out. Take the time to place boxes in their proper rooms. It will be easier to unpack properly once you get everything inside.

• **Keep one room free of boxes.** Okay, this suggestion does sort of contradict the previous one, but a box room will come in handy when you get overwhelmed and bogged down with all the unpacked stuff around you. This way, you'll have a clutter-free zone to escape from it all. Just don't scatter the boxes that belong in this room all over. Keep them as close as possible to the appropriate room so that you can move things right in when the time comes.

• **Create a file or folder for important moving notes and papers.** Keep your index cards here, as well as receipts, delivery information, inventory sheets, and any other documents you need for the move. Keep this folder in a safe place. This will save you the hassle of scrambling to find a particular document amid the chaotic moving process.

• **Let your kids help with the moving process.** Let them pack, label, and even physically move some of their own items. Not only will they be excited to help, but you'll be delegating some of the work that would otherwise take up your time. Just keep an eye on kids who are younger than 13, and make sure that you are the one who packs valuable and fragile items.

• **Designate a box to be unpacked first.** This should include items you'll need right away, such as toilet paper, soap, extra clothes, plastic plates, cups, utensils, scissors, cleaning products, and whatever else you think might come in handy on arrival. Load this box last so it's the first to be unloaded.

Basic Tools of the Trade

Who says clutter control has to be complex? There are many simple, inexpensive tools you can pick up just about anywhere to aid you in your quest for organization.

• **Hooks:** These tiny things come in many shapes and sizes, making them perfect for quick, easy organization solutions. Hang a hook in the kitchen or near the front door, and you have the perfect place to keep your keys. Hats, leashes, belts, bathrobes, bags, and umbrellas are all perfect for hook-hanging. Consider the smaller items you're always losing or searching for, and chances are, most of them will be right at home on hooks.

• **Containers:** These space-savers can work wonders all over your house, although they most often end up in closets. Use plastic bins, baskets, or even bags; just don't throw all sorts of stuff indiscriminately into the closest container you can find! Create systems that make sense by grouping things together appropriately. For example, store sweaters and winter clothing in plastic bins during the summer. Then they will be out of the way, neatly nestled, and free from moths, mildew, and mold. The easy access that containers create will cut back on a lot of your clutter confusion.

• **Literature Sorters:** Once you sort through your old newspapers, magazines, bill stubs, and junk mail, there are lots of things you can use to keep paper from piling up again. Magazine racks, mail and bill organizers, catalog binders, and carousel dividers will all make your life easier. Just don't allow all of these convenient, orderly sorters to tempt you into keeping unnecessary, useless paper.

• **Shelves:** Strategically placing some sturdy shelves in different areas of your home will help you to use and organize the space you have available in the best possible way. Use wall shelves to get items off the floor and out of the way, or try a few corner shelves, which fit nicely and make good displays.

Maintaining Clutter Control

As you begin to reorganize, redesign, clean up, and overhaul your home, make sure your hard work pays off. Unless you make an ongoing effort to keep your home clean and organized, you'll quickly discover it won't stay that way for long. Clutter will start to build up, and before you know it, you'll be back to where you started. Think carefully, therefore, about your daily habits and behaviors. Determine what needs to change to ensure that after your home is clean and organized, it stays this way.

If you live with roommates, a spouse, or an entire family, don't take on organizing and cleaning your home as an ongoing personal crusade. Solicit the help of the people you live with and insist on their support to maintain your efforts. Teach them to clean up after themselves, sort out (and even do) their own laundry, and put items back in their proper place when they're done using them.

Conquering Closet Clutter

WHETHER YOU LIVE IN A TINY APARTMENT with shoebox-sized storage space or a huge house with walk-in closets to die for, when you're struggling with clutter, closets are always a problem. Closets are the clutter bug's best friend—and worst enemy. Sure, you can shove whatever you want into them, shut the door, and then wipe your hands clean of the mess, but only temporarily. It always comes back to haunt you. (How many times have you opened your bedroom closet, only to have yet another shoebox, piled five levels high, slide off the shelf and hit you on the head?) If you're really serious about organizing your home, you have to be more mindful of what you're storing in your closets and arrange them carefully to free up additional storage space. Get your closets organized, and you'll breathe a tremendous sigh of relief when you can finally open the doors and easily find what you need.

Exploring Your Closets

Okay, so you know your closets are in serious need of an overhaul, but you're not sure how to get your act together. The easiest approach is to focus on one closet at a time or one room at a time. You might, for example, consider reorganizing all of the clothing closets in your bedrooms at the same time to make sure you store the right garments in the proper location.

All Clear!

To begin your closet exploration, choose a closet or a room and follow these basic steps. These suggestions for clearing out your closets use clothing closets as an example, but the same rules apply for any type of storage closet.

1. Before you start, determine what specific purpose the newly organized closet will have. Will you use it, for example, to store your everyday wardrobe, coats, and shoes, or for toys and sporting equipment?
2. Empty your closet.
3. Neatly lay out the contents on a nearby floor or open area and inventory all of the items.
4. Decide which items taken out of the unorganized closet actually belong in it and which items should be stored elsewhere.
5. Eliminate or discard anything that's damaged, outdated, not your style, or the wrong size.

The Replacements

After you toss the things you no longer need, decide whether or not you should replace any of them. Hold on now—this isn't license to go out and buy whatever you want. Clutter control means paring down, remember? So if you had a hard time throwing out that broken old pair of flip flops, and you have your heart set on seeking another pair, resist the urge if you still have twenty other perfectly good pairs of sandals to contend with in your closet. On the other hand, if you've just discarded three trash bags full of clothing that's no longer in style or doesn't fit anymore, you're probably going to have to replenish your wardrobe. If you do need to replace what you get rid of, make sure you allocate enough room in your closet for these new purchases. If you stuff your newly organized space to the gills now and then go to fit in your new items later, you're only going to clutter up your space all over again!

Maximizing Your Space

Once the closet's all clear and you can actually see the back wall for a change, determine how much room you have for closet organizers (discussed in the following section) by carefully measuring the empty closet. Round each measurement to the nearest 1/8", and make sure to be as accurate as possible. Write the measurements down as you take them, and check your work at least twice. When measuring a reach-in closet, determine the width of the closet by measuring the inside space between the two sidewalls, calculate the height by measuring from the floor to the ceiling, and gauge the depth from the distance between the inside surface of the face wall or door and the back wall. To measure a walk-in closet, determine the width of each wall, as well as the closet's height from floor to ceiling; don't forget to figure in the width and height of the doorway, too.

When you know exactly how much space you have to work with, evaluate the things you're keeping and determine the best way to store them. For example, would installing additional shelves, rods, or drawers give you some extra space? Most basic closets are equipped with a single rod for hanging clothing, but the closet's height usually allows for at least two rods. In essence, this doubles the amount of space you can use to hang garments. If your closet space is limited, you can make the most of the room you do have by using specially designed hangers to increase the number of garments you can hang in a smaller area of space.

■ ■ ■ ■ ■ Clutter Control Quickie: High Visibility

When organizing a clothing closet, keep your most-used items visible and easily accessible. According to Mary Lou Andre, the president of Organization By Design (800-578-3770, *www.dressingwell.com*), most people wear 20 percent of their wardrobes 80 percent of the time. These key items should be front-and-center. To further simplify things, preassemble some of your essential outfits, including accessories, and store them together on a single hanger. ■

Sort your hanging items by type or category. For example, divide up suits so that all jackets and skirts are together, then group jeans, dress pants, sweaters, and so on. Sort within each category by color and/or fabric type. Doing this will help you to create new outfit combinations by mixing and matching garments. You can also arrange your clothing by season, if it helps you to further organize things.

Finding the Right Hangers

When organizing any clothing closet, you need to have a variety of hangers. Before you decide which types will work best for you, get rid of all those bent and out-of-shape metal hangers you've built up over time, from trip after trip to the dry cleaner. Traditionally shaped wooden or plastic hangers are excellent for preserving virtually all of your hanging clothing, and they're much sturdier than thin metal hangers. Once you've made room for some new and improved models, choose hangers that are designed to hold specific types of garments. For example, use suit hangers, which are designed with a special pant rod, so a single hanger neatly holds both pants and a jacket. Cedar hangers have all the benefits of traditional wooden hangers, but also absorb moisture and discourage pests (such as moths) from damaging your clothing. And don't forget about collapsible, multitiered hangers—they save space by allowing you to hang several garments in one small area. Use your hangers strategically, and you can bet your clothes won't end up in a tangled mess or in a heap on the closet floor. Try any of the hanger solutions from the following companies, and you'll be on your way to a well-organized, clutter-free closet.

Hanger Handler, from Axiomatic Products Corporation (*www.hangerhandler.com*), holds up to thirty hangers and fifty pounds or more of garments. It hangs on closet rods, coat hooks, and over doors at home, and it prevents hanger tips from pressing into the palm of your hand, which makes it easier and more comfortable to transport multiple clothes hangers. It's handy for carrying dry-cleaning, traveling (with or without garment bags), and moving, but for your uncluttering purposes, it's especially useful when it comes to reorganizing closets—loading and unloading is easy because you can simply slide the Hanger Handler over hanger hooks. It's available for under $10 at The Container Store (888-266-8246, *www.containerstore.com*), select Bag 'n' Baggage retail stores, and Travel 2000 stores.

The Jam-It Slack Rack natural wood valet *(www.the storagestore.com)* and **The Hinge-It** invisible valet (*www.organize everything.com*) maximize space by mounting to a doorjamb or hinge. Both are easy to install and great for hanging clothes or towels.

Double Hang (*www.organizeeverything.com/doublehang.html*) will double the clothing hanging space in your closet. The heavy, natural wood bar (about the size of a closet rod) hangs on chrome-plated steel posts (it's 29.5" wide x 33.5" long).

The Round-A-Belt Organizer *(www.netwurx.net/~organize)* organizes up to forty belts into five different sections according to your personal style, making it easy to find the right belt and then remove it individually. No small feat, if it saves you from another frustrating morning search!

The Six Tier Multiple Blouse/Shirt Hanger (800-600-9817, *www.organizeeverything.com/6tiershirhan.html*) is a chrome hanger with a unique design that holds six shirts or blouses. This product is ideal for storing extra garments in a small space.

The Closet Carousel (800-896-0902, *www.closets.net*) is the ultimate organizational dream. It works much like a dry cleaner's clothing carousel, only it's been adapted and readied for home use in your own closet. The system operates with the push of a button, using ordinary household electricity. And since there are ten different standard models, it can be customized to fit in most closets, as long as there is a minimum of 4'6" x 6' space. It's equipped with easily adjustable single- or double-tier hanging racks; adjustable baskets for storing folded garments, handbags, and other accessories; and specially designed adjustable shoe racks.

The Quiet Power Motorized Tie Rack from Sharper Image (800-344-4444, *www.sharperimage.com*) also incorporates a carousel-like design, albeit smaller than that of a dry cleaner's. This battery-operated gadget organizes seventy-two neckties, which will glide quietly past you for easy selection (it also plugs into standard wall outlets with an AC adapter). A control bar allows you to rotate left or right in one full revolution or press stop when you've reached your selection. A bright light switches on automatically as the track rotates, then switches off once it stops. All this, and the oval track takes up only a 5¼" section of your closet rod—a clutter-control bargain by any standard!

You've probably seen TV infomercials for **Space Bags** (800-469-9044, *www.spacebag.com*), the large, heavy-duty plastic bags you shrink down using a vacuum cleaner to suck the air out of the plastic bag, thereby dramatically decreasing the space needed for storage. The airtight polyethylene and nylon seal is great for protecting things you need to store because it locks out water, moisture, mildew, dirt, bugs, and allergens. It also retards oxidation, which damages natural fibers and many synthetics. Once items are vacuum-packed in Space Bags, you can store them in your garage, attic, or basement, freeing up precious closet space in your home.

Considering Closet Organizers

Once you find the right hangers, you're well on your way to great closet clutter control. If you still need an extra boost, however, there are lots of inexpensive closet organizers that you can buy to finish the job in a snap. Many organizers fit easily into all sorts of closet types. Figure out which of the following combinations work best for you, and soon you'll have the closets of your dreams!

▨ ▨ ▨ ▨ ▪ **Clutter Control Quickie: Store Your Seasonals**

When cleaning and organizing your clothing closets, plan to store off-season clothing (laundered or dry-cleaned) elsewhere, such as in a separate closet, in boxes under the bed, or in your luggage. Include a cedar block in any box that contains wool garments. ▨

General Organizers

Check out any linen superstore, catalog, or Web site that features closet organizational products and you'll find a wide selection is available. These component-based storage systems allow you to customize the inside of your closets, without the high cost of hiring a professional to do the work. After you've measured your available closet space and know exactly what you want to store in your closet, you can design a closet-storage system that combines different modules. For example, the Hold Everything Catalog from Williams-Sonoma (800-421-2264, *www.williams-sonomainc.com*) offers stacking wooden drawers, cubes, and shelves that you can mix and match. This system can be joined with a closet's existing rod for hanging garments.

▨ ▨ ▨ ▨ ▪ **Clutter Control Quickie: Turn on the Lights**

If your closet is a mess because the lighting is poor and you can't find anything, try buying an inexpensive battery-operated light from the hardware store. Most mount easily to the wall with tape or small screws. For ideas, visit the eLights Web site at *www.elights.com*. Once you can actually see what you're doing, it will be a lot easier to keep your closet neat and clutter-free! ▨

Shelves and Shelf Dividers

Shelves save you by providing a place to put all those things you'd otherwise toss on the floor of your closet or stuff into a dresser drawer. Preassembled stackable shelves are a great choice—you can buy them at most home improvement or hardware stores, they're available in a variety of sizes, and they can be customized to fit the dimensions of your closet.

Shelf dividers separate your shelves into smaller sections that you use for securely stacking sweaters or stashing purses so that they don't tumble around and get damaged. Consider using other divider systems to organize socks, hosiery, jewelry, and folded linens.

Baskets

Use these versatile gems in closets anywhere you can. Ventilated baskets serve practically any purpose you can think of. Laundry baskets in bedroom closets make great portable hampers; baskets in kids' closets double as toy bins; and baskets in your foyer or mudroom closet are useful for storing gloves, hats, and sports gear or allowing damp outerwear to breathe and dry.

Canvas Storage Systems

These systems are ideal for storing off-season clothing. There are all sorts of hanging items available, including shoe holders, garment bags for coats and suits, shelves for sweaters, bedding bags for storing blankets and other large items, and even folding drawers for smaller items, such as scarves or socks. You can mix and match pieces to create your own ideal closet system.

Shoe Racks

A sturdy shoe rack is one of the best investments you can make when it comes to clearing the mess out of your closet. If you're stuck with a small closet, try a hanging shoe rack that you can attach to the back of the closet door, for example. The Hold Everything catalog (800-421-2264) features a wide selection of stackable wooden and metal shoe racks and shoe cabinets, as well as an Over-Door Storage System that frees up floor space.

■ ■ ■ ■ Clutter Control Quickie: Shoe Hang Ups

If you have more shoes than can fit comfortably on your closet floor or shelves, try a flexible, hanging shoe bag that attaches to the wall. The individual pouches make organizing shoes a breeze, and they also double as storage spots for your scarves, belts, or other small items, which will take some pressure off your dresser drawers. Make sure the pouches are transparent so that you can easily see exactly what's stored inside them. ■

Tie and Belt Racks

Ties and belts don't have to be strewn haphazardly all over your closet—find special holders and storage racks that can be attached to closet walls and doors or even hung from the closet's rod. Some racks also slide out when you need them and tuck away when you don't. Be sure to store tie racks close to dress shirts so that coordinating outfits is easy. Look for racks that have pegs with nubbed tips, to keep ties in place and prevent wrinkling.

Jewelry Organizers

Felt-lined jewelry organizers are a smart way to keep valuable and delicate possessions cushioned and protected. In some cases, a top tray slides and lifts out, giving you two layers of storage in a single drawer. Combinations of large and small compartments work for different types and styles of jewelry and accessories.

Customizing Your Closets

If you're handy with tools, you could opt to build your own closet organizers directly into the space that you have from scratch, to best suit your particular clutter control needs. Just be sure that if you go this route you think carefully about your plan to ensure that after you put in all that work, the end result functions properly. As you're planning your closet improvement project, think about these questions:

- How can you best change the appearance and organization of your closet to make it less cluttered and more functional?
- Is the space currently being used efficiently?
- Is there enough room to install drawers and/or cabinets with doors that open and close?
- Do you need more shelf room, hanging space, or drawers in the closet?
- Can you use your closet floor space and door properly right now, or are shoes and other things cluttering up the space?

Once you're ready to tackle a custom closet project, head to your nearest hardware superstore and find a do-it-yourself closet organizer kit that fits the specifications of your closet. A kit should include most of the materials you'll need. Just be sure to have some key tools handy, like a Phillips head screwdriver (a power screwdriver is even better), hammer, stud finder, level, tape measure, circular or fine-tooth saw, and pipe cutter or hacksaw.

If do-it-yourself home improvement just isn't your thing, you can always hire a professional closet organizer to do the job for you. There are many companies that will build custom rods, shelves, drawers, hooks, lighting, and other in-closet accessories designed specifically to fit the needs of your space. Many of these companies guarantee that their closet storage solutions will actually double your available storage, and in most cases, that is true. Be prepared to pay, though, because these services don't come cheap. If you do decide to enlist the skills of a professional closet organizer, here are a few good ones to investigate:

- California Closets (888-336-9709, *www.calclosets.com*)
- Closet Factory (800-692-5673, *www.closetfactory.com*)
- Techline (800-356-8400, *www.techlineusa.com*)
- Storage By Design (877-772-2313, *www.customclosets.com*)

Broadening Your Horizons

Smart closet organization is a key component for any uncluttered home, but closets can only take you so far. If your closet space is limited, you need to come up with alternative solutions to store all of your stuff properly. Before doing anything, figure out what items you need to store, how much noncloset storage space you have to work with, and what special precautions you need to take. Be organized and practical when devising alternative storage solutions, but also be conscious of what you're storing and what you need to do to ensure its safety. You might initially think, for example, that storing off-season clothing in cardboard boxes in your attic or basement is a good idea from a clutter-control standpoint, but not if those places aren't climate controlled. And there are other things to consider, such as the likelihood of unwanted pests like moths chewing through your good wool coats! After you've mulled over these sorts of scenarios, it will be easier for you to zero in on the right spots for storing your things.

Consider purchasing an armoire for out-of-season items or even as an extra closet space, if the closet in your bedroom is small. Check out the Armoires & More Web site (*www.armoire store.com*) or call 800-5-FURNISH to order the catalog, which features a broad range of styles. Or, if quick, inexpensive storage solutions are what you crave, Wal-Mart, Home Depot, Hold Everything, Bed, Bath & Beyond, the Container Store, Lillian Vernon, and lots of other places sell a variety of containers in all shapes and sizes that are safe for storing most types of clothing in the attic, basement, or garage. Also try Rubbermaid's Web site, *www.rubbermaid.com*.

▨ ▨ ▨ ▨ ▪ Clutter Control Quickie: Pull Your Weight

Installing shelving into your closets is a great way to save space—just make sure what you're storing isn't too heavy for the shelves. If the weight of books or other heavy items is too much for your shelves, they might collapse and create a dangerous situation. Install shelving carefully, so that it's properly affixed to walls. Many shelves list maximum weight capacities, so read carefully! ▨

After your closets are cleared and reorganized and you've found alternative spaces to catch the overflow, be sure to maintain your newfound storage solutions. Don't make the mistake of expanding your belongings to fill all of the newly available space. Focus on your needs and make a conscious effort to maintain the level of organization you have just worked so hard to achieve in your closets.

chapter 8
Clearing Your Kitchen

IS YOUR KITCHEN SUCH A DISASTER AREA that you can't even face cooking dinner at night? Read on, because no matter how many dirty dishes are piling up in your sink or how much old food is waiting to be dumped from your refrigerator, you can still take steps to create a well-organized, tidy kitchen. All it takes are some good cleaning tips and helpful storage solutions so that all your things are easy to find and readily available when you need them.

■ ■ ■ ■ ■ Clutter Control Quickie: Facing Your Food Clutter

If you're constantly throwing away uneaten food that has spoiled or you're loathe to open your refrigerator for fear of what might fall out, it's a sure sign of **food clutter**. Don't be a food hoarder—put more forethought into your grocery shopping, cooking, and food storage tactics. Cook only what you're sure you'll eat, to avoid leftover buildup, and before you add unnecessary items to your grocery list, double-check your cabinet stock first! ■

Taking Stock

If your current kitchen organization just isn't cutting it, do a quick walk-through and take stock of what's in every cabinet and drawer. Then, draw a small model of your kitchen and label where everything is currently located. Think about what you use each group of items for and consider if they are strategically placed in the areas most conducive to their purpose. If you never really considered it before, think now about how much time you spend walking back and forth across the kitchen—or sometimes even into a different room—to retrieve things. Now you get the picture, so draw your ideal placements for things into your model. Before you start ripping through your cabinets and drawers, ask yourself some questions.

- What do you like most and least about your kitchen's setup?
- Do you have enough counter space to prepare meals and store appliances?
- Is your kitchen sink large enough?
- Do you have enough refrigerator and freezer space?
- Is there enough storage space? Do you need more room for food, pots/pans, flatware, dishes, and so on?
- Do you have a system for organizing the things in your drawers and cabinets, or is everything simply thrown in wherever you can find some space?
- Do you have adequate shelf space?
- Can you adjust your cabinet shelves, and do your cabinet doors and drawers open easily?
- Aside from cooking, do you do other things in the kitchen, like pay bills, do laundry, use the computer, watch TV, and talk on the telephone?
- Do you need a bigger dish rack? If so, is there ample room for one?
- Do you need to make space on your counters for a cutting board?
- Where do you keep small kitchen items such as dish rags, towels, napkins, hand soap, and dish detergent? Are these little things hanging around all over your kitchen, creating extra, unnecessary clutter?
- Do you leave items that don't really belong in the kitchen, like keys, magazines, or mail, hanging around on counters just because you don't have a designated spot for them?
- What would you like to do in your kitchen area that you aren't able to do now?
- How would you ideally configure the seating area of your kitchen? Based on the space available, is there a more practical way to position your table and chairs?

Don't worry if you don't have the cash to go out and buy a bigger sink or renovate your cabinet space. Just by taking stock of what works and what doesn't, you can find ways to play up the good points and work around the drawbacks.

■ ■ ■ ■ ■ Clutter Control Quickie: Find the Right Dish Rack

If you're looking for an easier way to wash dishes, Williams Sonoma (877-812-6235, *www.williams-sonoma.com*) sells a stainless-steel dish rack designed with separate compartments for silverware, plates, bowls, mugs/glasses, and stemware. It's a cinch to keep clean and drains easily, so dishes dry quickly. If you live alone and don't use many dishes or utensils at one time, there's also a smaller version. ■

Once you assess your space, consider what types of storage improvements you can make. Where will you put everything in your reconfigured space? Can you come up with more organized methods for storing trays, cookie sheets, and other flat items? What about building taller shelves to hold wine glasses and vases? Is a recycling center important to you? If so, be sure to set aside the proper space so it doesn't get in the way of kitchen activity.

Just by asking yourself simple questions like these, you'll quickly zero in on which elements of your kitchen are most irksome to you. This recognition will help you to devise a game plan for tackling kitchen clutter.

■ ■ ■ ■ ■ Clutter Control Quickie: Think About How You Shop

As you unclutter your kitchen, it will help to think about your shopping habits. Do you typically shop for an entire week, or do you wing it day to day? Do you buy everything fresh or in bulk? What about nonperishables? How you answer these questions will affect the way you configure storage space. Think carefully, and write down organizational ideas based on these habits. ■

Your Kitchen Wish List

As you start to envision the setup of your ideal kitchen, create a kitchen wish list or scrap book, and fill it with ideas you see in magazines, stores, or on the Web. Also make a list of the most important things you want to keep in your kitchen, and include any you might need to add, because you'll need to figure out how to best use your space based on these items. Here are some examples:

- Adjustable shelving for food storage
- Bookshelf for cookbooks
- Breadbox
- Computer work area
- Cutlery storage area
- Divided silverware/flatware drawer
- Lazy Susan storage
- Microwave
- Better drawer storage
- More electrical outlets
- Recycling area
- Spice rack
- Television or radio

Freeing Countertops from Clutter

Whatever your end goals, clutter-free countertops will make a huge difference in the functionality of your kitchen. Take a look at what's on your counters right now. Is there anything that can be relocated into cabinets or onto shelves? Are there any small or medium-sized appliances you need to buy that will go on your counters?

▦ ▦ ▦ ■ Clutter Control Quickie: Easy Food Storage

Always use clear containers for storing food in the refrigerator so you can see exactly what's inside. Tupperware *(www.tupperware.com)* or Gladware *(www.gladware.com)* containers are ideal because they are airtight and go from the refrigerator or freezer, to the microwave, and then into the dishwasher. They're inexpensive, designed to maintain freshness, and easily stackable, so they'll really maximize your storage space. ■

Check to see if you can install some of your appliances, such as a microwave or television, under your cabinets. And instead of keeping your telephone on the counter, mount a cordless on a nearby wall. Even small things like rolls of paper towels take up room, so look for space-savers, like racks that hang on the wall or on the side of your refrigerator. Your kitchen will feel much less cluttered as soon as you get excess stuff off your countertops. Even if you don't have a lot of counter space, freeing up what you do have will give the illusion of more room.

Reconfiguring Cabinets and Drawers

In order to prevent clutter from rearing its messy head as you are cooking, eating, or doing whatever else you need to, all of your small utensils need to be properly separated, organized, and stored. And what about your nonperishable food items, pots and pans, dishes, glasses, appliances, cookbooks, and cleaning products? These also need proper homes.

Just as you did with your closets, when you organize your kitchen cabinets and drawers, empty everything out and take complete stock of what needs to be stored. Get rid of old items that are broken or unnecessary. Next, group all similar items together, such as canned goods, silverware, dishes, and so on, and determine how much storage space each set requires.

■ ■ ■ ■ ■ Clutter Control Quickie: Dish It Out

Dish racks are especially common areas for clutter to creep into your kitchen. Your dish rack should only be a temporary holding spot for things as they dry, not a final destination. Wash them, rinse them, and once they dry off, away they go! ■

Here are some suggestions for grouping your stuff:

- Baking tools
- Cleaning products
- Everyday dishes

- Everyday glasses and mugs
- Everyday silverware and flatware
- Formal dishes and fine china
- Formal silverware
- Kitchen linens (tablecloths, dish rags, napkins, and so on)
- Kitchen tools
- Pots and pans
- Serving dishes
- Small and medium-sized appliances
- Specialty items used for entertaining (cheese board, ice bucket, chip and dip plate, and so on)
- Pantry items (such as nonperishable food items)
- Wine glasses and formal glasses
- Wines bottles (opened and unopened)

After you divide your kitchen items into categories, determine whether each group needs cabinet space, drawer space, or some other type of storage. Do you need to keep all of these things right in the kitchen, or can some items, such as fine china, be kept in your formal dining area? Make sure you measure all of your available cabinet space so that you know the items will fit.

▪ ▪ ▪ ▪ ▪ Clutter Control Quickie: Keep Things Close

You'll save time if everything you need is within reach of your work area. For instance, keep plates, glasses, and silverware in the same vicinity, preferably close to the kitchen or dining room table. Mixing bowls, measuring cups, rolling pins, and so forth can be kept in cabinets above or close to the counter. And stovetop condiments such as salt, pepper, and oils can be placed in a cabinet above or next to the stove. ▪

Now consider how often you need to use each of these items. Start by putting the items you use less frequently at the back of cabinets that aren't as readily accessible. Then place the things that will be used often, such as your everyday silverware, plastic ware, mugs, and cups, in drawers or cabinets that are easier to access. Likewise, organize the pantry so that breakfast cereals, beverages, and other packaged foods are easiest to grab in a rush. Save a convenient space for other nonfood essentials, such as trash bags, napkins, plastic wrap, and foil, too.

▨ ▨ ▨ ▨ ▨ Clutter Control Quickie: Pot and Pan Placement

As a quick fix, overhead and wall-mounted pot/pan racks are great for storage and display—they save valuable cabinet space and keep pots and pans easily visible and within reach. Plus, if you're not constantly dragging those heavy things in and out of your cabinets, it saves a lot of wear and tear. ▨

Next, separate all of your kitchen tools from food and non-perishable items. Cleaning products, for example, can be kept under the sink, away from canned goods and pots and pans. Store products for dishwashing, mopping, stove polishing, and countertop cleaning in one convenient location. (If you choose to store them beneath the sink, use a safety lock to keep out curious toddlers.)

Devising Extra Drawer Space

You're probably already using a plastic or metal organizer for your silverware drawer to sort knives, forks, spoons, and other utensils, but there are many types of organizers available to help you unclutter other small kitchen items. Kitchens, Etc. (800-232-4070, *www.kitchenetc.com*), for example, offers twenty-eight different styles. Once you figure out which items need to be stored within each drawer, you can determine the size of the individual compartments you'll use to split the drawer space. Bear in mind that some items, such as knives and cutlery, require special storage to keep them from getting dull or damaged. If you don't have enough space for a hardwood knife block on top of your counter, a magnetic wall-mounted knife rack/utensil holder might be a more practical choice.

■ ■ ■ ■ ■ Clutter Control Quickie: Pull Some Strings

Lots of people stick mops, brooms, pails, and dustpans anywhere they can squeeze a bit of space in their kitchen, like in that narrow slit next to the fridge. This looks messy and adds to kitchen clutter. Instead, keep these items in a closet. For easy access, screw some small metal hooks to the inside of the closet door, and tie a loop of thin yarn to each item, so that you can hang them up and grab them quickly when you need them. ■

Organizing Your Refrigerator and Freezer

This is one task nobody likes to tackle, but it's got to be done, so roll up your sleeves, plug your nose, and grin and bear it. The first step is emptying your refrigerator and freezer in order to clean the appliance itself. Remove all of the shelves and wash them thoroughly. Start on the top shelf, and work your way down. Open all containers and check what's inside. Decide which things will be kept, and then throw away old leftovers, anything that's moldy, and all the stuff you know you'll never eat. Don't cut corners here—check the expirations on all dated items, and toss anything that's out of code or questionable. There's no sense keeping anything that's just taking up space.

■ ■ ■ ■ ■ Clutter Control Quickie: Replenishing Your Stock

As you're reorganizing your refrigerator and freezer, keep track of what you're throwing out and what you need to replace. Create a shopping list of these items as you go along, and you'll be a step ahead when you finish. ■

Next, inventory the remaining items and decide how you'll organize them. Take full advantage of the drawers, shelves, and refrigerator door. Designate certain shelves for particular items, and keep similar items, such as drinks, together. Store small loose items and leftovers in clear plastic containers (so that you can see what's inside).

Clipping Coupons Efficiently

Instead of leaving coupons all over the place and then throwing them into your purse every time you run to the store, try using a small, portable binder with clear pockets to sort, categorize, and store coupons. Label each pocket as a separate category, such as "Cleaning Products" or "Pet Care," then group all related coupons together. Another alternative is to use a small file box and store your coupons alphabetically, by product name or brand. Or, if you have a PDA, start using it to keep track of your grocery list. Because a PDA is totally portable, it's perfect to carry with you into the supermarket.

■ ■ ■ ■ ■ Clutter Control Quickie: The Spice Is Right

Spice racks are convenient in the kitchen because they save you the time of having to dig through a cabinet where lots of little jars are scattered haphazardly. Rather than sticking the jars absentmindedly into any spot on your spice rack, try alphabetizing the individual containers. This way, you'll always know that your chives are right next to your cinnamon. ■

As a general rule, clip and store coupons for only those products you already use (or definitely want to try). Also pay attention to the expiration date and the fine print on the coupons you clip. If you clip a coupon on Sunday, but know you won't go food shopping for at least a week and the coupon will expire, don't bother saving it. And never let your coupon clipping contribute your clutter habit. Before you go crazy at the store and buy up everything for which you have a coupon, think about whether you have the space to store all of these extra bulk items. There's no sense buying two extra-large containers of laundry detergent with a coupon if you don't have ample room to store the stuff!

■ ■ ■ ■ ■ Clutter Control Quickie: Create a Coupon List

Save yourself time and frustration by adding notes about your coupons to your shopping list. Place a star or some other notation next to any items you have coupons for, then list the specific name brands and sizes you need to purchase next to the item. ▨

Organizing Recipes

If cooking is your strong suit, chances are you've acquired many recipes over time from cookbooks, magazines, friends, relatives, and the Internet. But loose recipes scattered in different places all over your kitchen won't do you any good. You need to control recipe clutter as well! One useful way to store recipes is in clear, protective plastic sheets that you can put into a three-ring binder with dividers. Separate the binder into sections, such as "Appetizers," "Desserts," "Chicken Dishes," and so on. Keep this binder with your cookbooks, on a shelf in the kitchen, and you'll save yourself the hassle of scouring your shelves and drawers for loose recipes.

You could also file your recipes in a filing cabinet or, better yet, if you're tech savvy, try creating a recipe filing system on your computer. There are several electronic cookbook computer software packages on the market, or you could use a database management program to create your own system for filing your recipes.

▨ ▨ ▨ ▨ ▨ Clutter Control Quickie: Soak Your Dishes

Keep your sink full of soapy water while cooking, and when you finish with an item, slide it right into the sink. If you do this with each utensil and dish you use, when you're done cooking, all you'll need to do is wipe and rinse the dishes. Of course, if you're fixing a six-course meal for several guests, you might have to keep replenishing clean soapy water. But for smaller meals, this technique will save you time and energy. ▨

A personal digital assistant, such as the Handspring Visor (*www.handspring.com*) or Palm *(www.palm.com),* can also be used as a handheld electronic recipe storage system. CookBook *(www.dovcom.com/cookbook.html)* is an easy-to-use database that allows you to store your favorite recipes on the Palm PDA device for quick reference in the kitchen. The program features basic editing tools, such as cut, copy, and paste, as well as a Find feature, and it has fifteen user-defined categories, which should be enough to keep your recipes organized and uncluttered.

Dealing with Trash and Recyclables

Out of all the rooms in your home, the kitchen is probably where the majority of your trash is created and collected. If you don't have a good system for handling all of this garbage, it's sure to clutter up your kitchen. An organized trash and recycling system will help you to keep all sorts of clutter, such as newspapers or empty boxes, from piling up all around your house. Here are some quick tips from Glad Products Company for creating an efficient disposal system in your kitchen:

• A large, streamlined stainless-steel garbage can is the easiest to keep all of your trash under control. Choose a model that has a foot-lever to open the garbage can's lid. This way, you won't have to touch it with your hands, which is more convenient and sanitary.

• If your recyclables aren't organized, they can make a mess out of your kitchen. Use small bins lined with waste-basket bags to separate recyclables like aluminum, plastic, newspaper, and glass. This will help to keep kitchen clutter to a minimum.

• Steel, glass, and aluminum are easy to recognize and recycle. Be sure not to mix glass bottles with other types of glass, such as mirrors or glass tableware. If you separate items properly in your kitchen, you won't create a huge mess.

• Rather than allowing magazines, junk mail, old takeout menus, and other paper products to pile up all over your house, round up all of your clean, dry, and uncontaminated paper products for recycling as soon as you are done with them.

▦ ▦ ▦ ▦ ▦ Clutter Control Quickie: Create a Family Message Center

If you want to cut down on time clutter for your entire family, designate a place in the kitchen, such as the refrigerator, to be your family's message center. Hang a large corkboard or dry erase board for posting messages, notes, and schedules, as well as several small bins for sorting each individual's mail. You can keep your food-shopping list here, too, so that all members of the family can add to it as needed. ▦

chapter 9

Creating a Comfortable Living Room or Family Room

IN MANY HOMES, the living room is the first room everyone sees when entering the front door, and that first impression means a lot. The living room is a place where good memories are made and preserved. From family pictures on the mantel to that fabulous ottoman you reupholstered yourself, your living room should represent the harmony you have in all of your relationships and activities. Remember, the living room is for living, not for burying yourself in the debris of your life!

Optimal use of space is key in your family room, since it is the center of energy and activity in your home. Because it sets the tone for the rest of your house, it's especially important that your living area be easily accessible from other rooms. If clutter is creeping up around your living room space, you need to clear it out to improve the general flow and function of your home. The same holds true for your den, family room, or great room, especially if your home doesn't have a "formal" living room. All of these rooms have an inherent family energy and should be organized and decorated to promote a hospitable and inviting living environment.

Recognizing Your Needs

Depending on the size of your home and your habits, your living area can have many uses. Because of this, storage in the living area can be a tricky thing. If your household is a busy one and your living area is a prime traffic zone, it's probably also the drop-off spot for all sorts of items vying for their fair share of uncluttered space.

▓ ▓ ▓ ▓ ▓ Clutter Control Quickie: Pulling Double Duty

For items that don't necessarily need to be displayed, consider a coffee table with drawers beneath it or an ottoman that doubles as a storage box. Don't forget that chests and armoires aren't only for the bedroom. If you have the space, these are great in the living room because they often feature multiple shelves or closed cabinets for storing things other than clothes, such as board games, video game systems, blankets, CDs, or DVDs. ▓

More than likely, you spend a great deal of time in your living area, so you want to ensure that it's as comfortable and clutter-free as possible. One good way to figure out how to best organize your living room is to keep a journal of the things you like to do there and the various items you need to store in your living room related to these activities. This will tell you most clearly what kind of space you need to create.

Starting with the basics, think about exactly what you use (or want to use) your living room for. Next, determine what furniture and other fixtures you need in order to accommodate these activities. For example, if the living area is where your family relaxes and watches television, you need a well-organized entertainment center and plenty of comfortable seating, along with a coffee table and/or end tables. If this is the room where your art collection or collectibles are stored and displayed, you need to accommodate those items with adequate wall space, shelves, or display cabinets, so that the items don't appear too cluttered. Or, if you enjoy curling up on a chilly evening to read a book in front of the fire, plan the space around your fireplace properly to accommodate the various tools you'll need.

▓ ▓ ▓ ▓ ▓ Clutter Control Quickie: Keep Things Portable

When purchasing furniture and other items for a small living space, always think fold-up, pull-out, and multipurpose. For example, a fold-out table can be used for eating and also function as a desk; an armoire is good for storage, but can also serve as a computer workstation; and a couch-futon can be used to sleep at night, but double as a sofa during the day. ■

Consider alternate uses for the room as well. If, for example, you install a sofa bed in the room, can it double as a guest room when people plan to stay over? Will this room also be used as a part-time home office? If so, what additional furniture (such as a desk and file cabinets or computer workstation and extra phone jacks) will you need? Once you consider your room's various uses, you'll be able to figure out how to maintain the proper balance of comfort and functionality in your living area without overcluttering the room.

Before clearing all of the little things that clutter your living area or family room, think strategically about the big pieces of furniture you have. Remember, when it comes to furniture, less is always more. Placing too much furniture within the room, no matter how fancy or comfortable you want it to be, will only create an overcrowded look and detract from the functionality of your space, so make sure you're dealing only with the essentials. Sometimes, simply rearranging the furniture you do have into a more functional design helps to alleviate clutter. Also make good use of any alcoves or recessed walls you have by lining them with shelves to create additional storage and display space.

■ ■ ■ ■ ■ Clutter Control Quickie: Reduce Coffee Table Clutter

If your coffee table is crowded with all sorts of electronic remote controls, invest in a multifunctional universal model and rid yourself of separate remotes for your TV, cable box, VCR, DVD, surround-sound system, and stereo. Or, at the very least, use a remote control caddy to help you keep track of them all. The Frontgate catalog (888-263-9850, *www.frontgate.com*), for example, offers several different remote control caddies. ■

Once you configure your sofa, love seat, chairs, and tables in a way that's conducive to your lifestyle, next you need to focus on other large items that suck up space and breed clutter in your living room, namely your electronics and computer paraphernalia.

Arranging Your Entertainment Center

Maximizing the storage space in your entertainment center isn't necessarily an easy task. When reorganizing a wall unit or entertainment center, first inventory all of the electronics that you must store on/in it. Be sure that the piece of furniture you have has ample room for your television, cable box, DVD player, VCR, stereo, video game system(s), surround-sound system, speakers, and any other electronics. If possible, keep your entertainment center in a spot that is close to electrical outlets and a phone jack, so that you don't have to deal with a jumble of cords and wires running every which way across your room.

▪ ▪ ▪ ▪ ▪ Clutter Control Quickie: Making Space for Electronics

In the case of extremely limited living room space, consider mounting your TV, VCR, and stereo on a wall using specially made brackets. This will free up floor space, which will help you to create a more open feeling in a living space that is small. The Frontgate catalog (888-263-9850, *www.frontgate.com*) offers several different wall-mounted media centers and TV pedestals. ▪

Once you're satisfied with the placement of your entertainment center/wall unit, start gathering up all those odds and ends you've got strewn all over your family room. No more videos left lying out on the coffee table, no more CDs piled on your desk. Think about how to best organize your audio and video electronics. Don't cut corners here—take the time to sort through all those DVDs and video games, and fit them into their own easily accessible places so that you're not tempted to rifle through them all and make a disorganized mess out of everything. Also label all of the wires associated with each piece of equipment, using tape or a Brother P-Touch label maker (available from any office supply store). Or, if you're feeling particularly ambitious, use different colored ties to wrap related wires together for easy identification.

If you can't fit all of the things you need to in your entertainment center, additional, smaller display racks and organizers that hold your entire CD, DVD, or video game collections are a must. Tall, slender freestanding units are great space savers, because you can fit them into unused corners and optimize slivers of available space.

Keeping Up with Your Computer Area

Many people keep their computer in the living area. It's important to set up a station that is conducive to working, yet doesn't take up too much space or add unnecessary clutter to your living room. First off, make sure you have a computer workstation or desk that offers ample space for your entire computer system (including printer, scanner, modem, and so on), while still allowing enough room to spread out your papers and work comfortably. Lack of desk space can easily lead to clutter pileups around your computer, and that's the last thing you want to infringe on a place where you and your family spend time relaxing.

■ ■ ■ ■ ■ Clutter Control Quickie: The Flip Side of Clutter

If you have a formal living room, it might be the one room in your house that is relatively uncluttered—especially if you reserve it for special occasions, such as holidays or visits from friends and family. Just don't be one of those people who vigilantly guards her furniture or fearfully hovers over guests every time they enter the living room. Clutter control is admirable, but it's just as bothersome if you prevent people from living comfortably within your space! What's the use of spending lots of time and money decorating a living room if you can't even do any *living* in it? ■

Most office supply stores, such as Staples (*www.staples.com*, 800-3STAPLE) have inexpensive home office units to make the most of your computer area, including styles that fit nicely into corners without overtaking your living space. Ikea, which has retail stores across America, as well as a mail-order catalog and a Web site *(www.ikea-usa.com)*, also offers a wide selection of innovative and highly functional living room furniture selections that are extremely economical. (See Chapter 14 for more information on setting up a home office.)

Closable office centers, such as the ones offered by Hold Everything (800-421-2264, *www.holdeverything.com*), are a great way to curtail computer clutter and keep your work space organized and separated from your living space. These cabinets are usually hardwood and offer a pullout keyboard tray, drawers, and room for a 19" monitor, CPU, and other accessories. Some models have doors with dry-erase boards or metal memo holders, as well as built-in magazine/file racks.

Knowing Your Boundaries

If you keep your computer in the living area, be especially mindful not to mix business with relaxation. It's amazing how quickly excess books, files, and computer paraphernalia can creep in and root themselves in your living room. Whether you realize it or not, these work-related things might be disturbing the peace by blurring boundaries and adding a feeling of chaos, which can seriously disrupt your living space and your family life.

Periodically check around your living room to be sure there are no stray work papers, files, or sticky notes that will get between you and your quality family time. You might also want to move the sofa and chairs into a square or octagonal position to foster a sense of closeness and sharing—and to keep outside influences from entering this important space. It's much harder to bring your work into the living room when the furniture is arranged in this manner. If you absolutely must use the space in your living room as an office sometimes, be sure either to section your desk area off with a screen or some plants, or to buy a desk with cupboards that totally enclose the work space. This way, none of your work stuff will be visible when you are using the living room for its primary purpose. Whatever you do, just make sure you respect the boundaries of your living room and, whenever possible, prevent your work from invading that space!

Displaying Artwork and Collectibles

If you're the type of clutter bug who loves collectibles, you're probably struggling to organize tabletops and shelves that are covered with all sorts of knickknacks. Resist the urge to turn your living room into an unruly trinket town. You don't have to do away with your special collections of artwork, statues, or memorabilia, but you do need to think carefully about what to do with them, especially if space is limited. Begin by going through your collection and throwing away items that are broken or that you no longer wish to keep. Be honest with yourself as you're doing this—do you really have a great emotional attachment to that chintzy little ceramic statue you won at the amusement park who knows how many years ago, or are you just holding on to it out of habit?

■ ■ ■ ■ Clutter Control Quickie: Things Are Looking Up

If you've packed too much clutter into a small living space, think vertical. The most underused space in any room is the 2' or 3' just below the ceiling. In the living room, use this space for knickknacks, books, and other small items. Consider using taller book shelves, and, if you can, mount shelves high up on the walls or over windows and doors. ■

Next, sort through the items you do want to keep, and decide on which ones you don't necessarily need to display every day. Seasonal knickknacks are perfect for this type of space saving. Just make sure to pack all related items together and label things carefully. That way, when next spring rolls around, you won't mistakenly pull out your Halloween jack-o-lanterns and scarecrows when you're looking for Easter eggs and bunnies!

Above all, when reorganizing your collectibles, don't create displays that look cluttered. Too many knickknacks in too little space is never visually appealing. Plan the best method to display whatever items you want to show off, and consider grouping similar items together.

Creating well-lit, deliberate displays will help you in your battle against clutter. According to some interior designers, the secret to elegant displays is lush layering. Begin with one tall object placed in the center of the collection, then loosely create a triangle shape as you work down to the display surface (such as the tabletop or shelf). If the items need wall space, consider filling a blank wall with multiple items in a similar theme. By artistically positioning similar frames, you'll add to the overall cohesiveness of your displays, which will further squelch that dreaded feeling of disorganized clutter.

In a Book Bind?

Perhaps more than any other item in your house (besides clothes, shoes, and handbags, that is) books seem to propagate mysteriously when you're not watching. Many of your books are probably stacked on tables and on the floor, next to your bed or favorite chair. Although you might derive great comfort being surrounded by books, you probably don't enjoy tripping over them or having to hunt one of them down. Bibliophiles (yes, you, too—you are reading a book right now, after all) can also benefit from a good dose of clutter control.

▪ ▪ ▪ ▪ ▪ Clutter Control Quickie: Beware of Book Bulk

Uncluttering your books can be a hefty proposition. Books are bulky and they take up lots of space. Whether you have freestanding bookcases or you decide to build extra shelves directly into the walls, be sure to consider the weight of your books and ensure that the shelving/bookcase can hold this excessive heaviness. ▪

To create a well-organized personal library, begin by sorting through your entire collection. Weed out books you no longer want and consider giving them away to friends or donating them to a local library. Next, sort your books by category (fiction, nonfiction, short stories, poetry, plays, travel, religious, how-to, children's books, textbooks, and so on). Determine how much bookcase or shelf space you need, and then try these suggestions for organizing your books:

• **By category:** Texts relating to your work can be kept in your office, or books relating to your hobbies can be shelved near where you engage in those hobbies. Store cookbooks in the kitchen, contemplative books in the sunroom, and entertainment books in the den.

• **By personal connection:** Keep the books that are most nostalgic, comforting, and interesting to you in your bedroom.

• **By alphabet:** Some people swear by this method. Individuals have been known to extend this approach to other things, like medicine bottles in their bathrooms. If you find this approach relaxing, by all means, knock yourself out! But if this method will only cause you stress, or, worse, lead you to delay the whole project because of the time involved, then go a different route.

• **Get rid of books that no longer serve you:** Have some good books that really helped you through a rough time in your life, but which you no longer need? Consider giving them to someone you know who might benefit from their wisdom—or sell them at an online auction or garage sale. Give old books new life!

Be sure to reserve some space at the edge of your shelves. Once you've shelved everything, you can use small bookstands to display special items, like your family scrapbook. Decorative book ends are another great way to add a personal touch to your home library. They also help to keep things neat and uncluttered by preventing books from falling over. You might also want to place a few of your trinkets on your book shelves—just be sure not to over clutter!

▦ ▦ ▦ ▦ ▪ Clutter Control Quickie: Move Those Magazines

Resist the urge to pile all of your magazines onto bookshelves. Magazines should be displayed separately, on a coffee or cocktail table, or in a free-standing rack. You might also be able to find end tables with built-in shelves that can be used for storing magazines, as well as other items like books and remote controls. ▪

Organizing Photographs

In many homes, the living area is also a central location for displaying family photos, but wall and mantle space will only take you so far. Once you've utilized all your free photo space, that's when random envelopes of photos start to creep up all over. Next thing you know, you have no idea where to find photos of the kids when they were small or what happened to those great shots you snapped while on vacation. Don't get swallowed up by your photo mess; devise a way to organize prints and negatives and then be consistent with your system. Even if you don't put all of your pictures into photo albums every time you develop a roll of film, at least be sure to label your prints and negatives and store them all in one location so that you can easily keep track.

While organizing your photos, keep these tips from the Graceful Bee NewBees Web site in mind:

- Use acid-free labels and acid-free permanent pen to document your negatives with the date and a description of the subject matter.
- Keep a film log of all the photos you take.
- Store photographs in resealable bags.

For normal storage in climate-controlled areas, cardboard, wooden, or leather boxes designed for storing photos work well. (If you're on a tight budget, you can even use shoe boxes.) When you store photos and memorabilia in an attic, garage, or other non-climate-controlled area, however, the photos should be kept in airtight plastic containers so they stay safe and well preserved. In any case, just make sure you properly label each box for easy identification.

■ ■ ■ ■ ■ Clutter Control Quickie: Start Scrapbooking

If you've reviewed and organized all of your photos and find you have some extra ambition to take it a step further, choose your favorites and create photo albums or scrapbooks around particular themes, such as family vacations, holidays, or family memories. For ideas on how to personalize and organize your scrapbooks, check out Scrapbooking.com *(www.scrapbooking.com)*, Scrapbook Tips.com *(www.scrapbook-tips.com)*, or AlbumSource.com *(www.albumsource.com)*. ■

Converting to Digital Photos

If you're really gung ho about controlling the photo clutter you've accumulated, consider converting to an entirely digital system that stores photos electronically. You can scan your existing photos to create high-resolution electronic files on your computer's hard drive, on Zip disks (from Iomega), or on writable CD-ROMs. The Hewlett-Packard Photo Smart Photo Scanner, for example, is relatively inexpensive and allows you to scan photos, negatives, or slides using any PC-based personal computer. You can also edit and touch up electronic images using special software, such as Microsoft's PhotoDraw program.

America Online's "You've Got Pictures" service is another way someone with little or no computer literacy can create electronic images from their photographs, organize these images, and store them. This service allows you to take 35mm film to a photo developer as you normally would and also fill in your AOL screen name so that AOL can e-mail you electronic versions of your printed photos within forty-eight hours.

Adding Tranquility to Your Living Room

No matter what tactics you use to shape up this space in your home, the bottom line is that your "room for living" should reflect who you are—or at least who you'd like to see yourself become, if you're trying to reform your clutter-bug ways. It should be a place that is conducive to relaxing, being calm and comfortable, and enjoying time with family and friends. Here are some easy feng shui tips to help you boost the tranquility and harmony level in your living room:

* In feng shui, the best energies for a living room come from the south, southeast, or southwest. These directions inspire creativity, lively conversation, and the positive exchange of ideas, so make the most of those areas
* Position furniture so that it supports the main purpose of the room, which is building a strong sense of family cohesiveness. Sofa and chairs should be arranged so they face the center of the room. Also remember that no one should be seated with their back to an entrance or window—you don't want your guests to feel open and vulnerable.
* Soften the harsh edges of end tables and coffee tables by angling more rounded pieces of furniture in a way that cushions or supports those sharper objects.
* Make sure the layout of your furniture is as well balanced as possible.
* Use plenty of warm colors, soft fabrics such as velvet or chenille, and cozy accessories like soft pillows and blankets in your living room.
* Boost the positive energy in your living room with bright,

colorful artwork. If you want to further soften the room or enhance its peaceful qualities, use pastels.

• Appeal to the senses: Aromatherapy items such as scented candles, oils, or potpourri engage the sense of smell; soft music or a water fountain capture the sense of sound; and various types of lights grab the sense of sight.

• Group family photos together on your mantle or, if you don't have a mantle, carve out a small space for photos on a table or shelf.

Ideally, a well-balanced living room contains an invigorating mix of colors, shapes, and textures—a healthy dose of yin and yang opposites. Most of all, balance everything in a way that instantly creates a feeling of calm in the room. Remember, the living room is a room for peaceful relaxation as much as it is a room for warm gatherings with family and friends. When you create order and balance in this room, you create harmony in your life—and that extends to the life of your family, too.

chapter 10

Arranging a Spacious Dining Area

WHETHER YOU EAT EVERY MEAL in your dining area or reserve it for festive holiday celebrations and dinner parties, this is a room where your family and friends gather to enjoy good food and time spent together. A cluttered dining area does not lend itself to the sort of relaxed, easy environment you want to create. If you can't make heads or tails out of your fine china or your good silverware is scattered all over the place, read on and learn how to create a dining room that is well organized and enables you to entertain smoothly.

Determining Your Needs

As with all the other rooms in your home that need to be reorganized, the first step involves determining what your needs are. Answer the following questions:

- What is the primary use of your dining area? (Casual dining with your family? Formal dining with friends, family, and/or business associates? Storage? Will this room double as a place for you to do work or your kids to do homework?)
- How often will you use the dining area for dining? (Nightly, weekly, monthly, once a year? Only for holidays?)
- How often will the dining area be used for activities other than dining?
- How many people do you typically need to accommodate in your dining area? There's a big difference between using your dining area to accommodate a family of four each night and using it several times a year to host Thanksgiving and Christmas dinner for your entire extended clan!

Storage Options

The primary consideration when organizing your dining area is the table. Dining room tables often take up a lot of space, and you need to situate the rest of the stuff in your dining room wisely, based on your table's size. If you're lucky enough to have a dining room table that can be expanded by adding leaves, you've got the best of both worlds, because you can keep it smaller when you don't have company, in order to save space, but then also expand it when you have guests, so that people aren't cramped in tight quarters.

▪ ▪ ▪ ▪ ▪ Clutter Control Quickie: Keep It Separated

If you're a clutter bug who throws all sorts of things into the dishwasher without a second thought, think again. Never put silver and stainless steel flatware in the same basket section—the metals should not touch each other. When washing your fine flatware, use only warm, sudsy water and avoid using harsh dishwashing detergents that contain chlorides or acids, such as lemon-scented detergents. Then hand-dry silver, especially knife blades, to avoid spotting and pitting. ▪

Beyond your dining room table and chairs, think about what you store in this area. Do you have the appropriate shelves or glass cabinets to display knickknacks and fine china, or are things scattered about in various places? Would it make more sense if you had separate drawers in your dining area to store your table linens, fine flatware, and those larger serving dishes that don't fit in your kitchen cabinets? As you've done with other items in other rooms, take an inventory of your china, formal flatware, large serving pieces, and table linens to determine how much drawer space, shelf space, and cabinet space you need to organize things properly. Remember to store similar items together in groups! It won't do you any good to stuff everything under the sun into the cabinets under your hutch if it's all so disorganized you can't even figure out what you have!

Also consider other items related to your dining area. Where do you keep your wine bottles, for example? Do you have to run downstairs to the basement, garage, or elsewhere to grab them every time you have visitors? If so, you might want to consider purchasing a small wine rack for your dining room. Many types of stores offer styles that take up very little space and also add an attractive touch to your room. For starters, try the Linens 'n Things or Bombay Company Web sites (*www.lnt.com* and *www.bombaycompany.com.*)

■ ■ ■ ■ ■ Clutter Control Quickie: Proper Silverware Storage

If you have expensive formal flatware, you shouldn't be lax about storing it! Don't leave it scattered among your everyday flatware, in a crowded kitchen cabinet; invest in a multicompartment flatware tray, chest, or storage box with an antitarnish lining. First consider functionality and organizational ease, then consider how the item fits into the overall décor of your room. Check out the Western Silver Company (800-850-3579, *www.westernsilver.com)* for information on purchasing and storing silverware. ■

Before you go crazy and get all sorts of new pieces for your dining room, make a detailed list of what, exactly, you want to add to your dining area. Then measure the room carefully and sketch out the placement of each item. You don't want to add pieces you think will help you to unclutter the room, only to find they take up so much space your clutter gets worse! As you're measuring, don't forget to consider the size of the dining room table when it's fully expanded. Also make sure you leave room for people to pull out their dining room chairs in order to stand up or sit down, and leave some space to walk around.

■ ■ ■ ■ ■ Clutter Control Quickie: Room to Breathe

As you're controlling dining room clutter, it's an excellent idea to find appropriate storage solutions for good table linens. Just refrain from storing fine linens in their original plastic packaging. A plastic container or bag will trap moisture and bacteria, which could eventually cause discoloration. Also, don't keep your table linens in overcrowded drawers—if you have to fold fabric very tightly, it will crease and damage over time.

If having a full-sized dining room set would add too much clutter to your room, but you still occasionally want to have formal dinner parties in your home, you can transform a standard folding card table into an eight-person dining table using a padded table topper. Look into the one offered in the Solutions catalog (800-342-9988, *www.solutionscatalog.com)*, which features the 48" Round Card Table Extender (item #63586) or the 54" Round Card Table Extender (item #63587). The deluxe ⅝" thick padding features a vinyl top and woven polyester bottom that won't scratch your table. Special side straps secure this tabletop to the table legs to prevent slipping. The best part about it is that it's priced under $90 and folds flat for storage, which will help you on your clutter-control crusade. Just add a nice tablecloth, fine china, and some candles, and you've instantly created a formal dining experience without having a large formal table cluttering your space every day.

▪ ▪ ▪ ▪ ▪ Clutter Control Quickie: Don't Leave Your Leaves Out

When not in use, keep the leaves from your dining room table out of the way, in a place that won't add to your clutter, such as against the back wall of a nearby closet. To keep them from getting damaged, wrap a towel around each leaf as you place it against the closet wall. ▪

As for your dining room chairs, the most important thing is making sure you don't cram too many chairs into a space that's too small. In terms of sizing, a typical dining room chair measures around 22" wide. Most interior design experts suggest leaving at least 12" to 18" of space between each chair. This gives the people sitting down ample elbow room. Also, when considering your available space, try to leave at least 20" to 30" between the back of each chair and the nearest wall or door. This provides plenty of room for people to move around. If you find you have too many formal chairs cluttering up a small area of dining room space, you might want to consider storing extra chairs elsewhere and then bringing them into the dining room only when needed. Just make sure you don't store good pieces of furniture in places like the attic or basement, where poor climate control could damage delicate wood or fabric. Another solution might be keeping just a few formal chairs to go with your table and then filling in with portable folding chairs in a pinch.

■ ■ ■ ■ ■ Clutter Control Quickie: The Simpler, The Better

When decorating your dining area, simple elegance is always better. Don't allow your room to fill up with all sorts of odds and ends that can't find homes anywhere else; excess clutter will detract from the overall décor of your room. Instead, highlight your fine table linens and china, play up a single beautiful flower arrangement or candle holder on the center of your table, and set off your atmosphere with beautiful mood lighting. ■

Protecting Your Fine China

If you choose to display your fine china in a cabinet, it will be well protected behind closed glass doors. But what if you don't have room for a china cabinet or can't afford one at this point? If you need to store your fine china in drawers or closed cabinets, take steps to protect these expensive, fragile items properly. Quilted cases are perfect for china because they help to keep dust away and also prevent chipping and scratching. Bed Bath & Beyond (*www.bedbathandbeyond.com* or 800-462-3966) offers several different styles, such as a set of four round keepers that hold twelve dinner plates, dessert plates, salad plates, or saucers.

■ ■ ■ ■ ■ Clutter Control Quickie: Add Some Highlights

Once you eliminate unnecessary clutter from your dining area, you should settle on just a few accent pieces that enhance your room. If, for instance, you have artwork to showcase in your dining area or you want to display a statue on a shelf, add drama to and focus interest by using accent lighting. Direct more intense light levels onto artwork or sculptures with directional wall, ceiling, or recessed fixtures. ▪

To prevent chips and scratches while storing china in these cases, be sure to place a separate soft foam protector between each item. You can also purchase dinnerware storage pouches, manufactured from quilted cotton with acrylic felt inserts and zippered tops, from Old China Patterns Limited by calling 800-663-4533 or by visiting the company's Web site *(www.chinapatterns.com)*. Once secured properly, these cases can then be safely stored out of the way, in a drawer or cabinet.

Stocking Your Liquor Cabinet

Whether you have a stand-alone liquor cabinet or a wine rack built into your buffet or credenza, keeping all of your related supplies together in one area is a clutter control must. In addition to the actual bottles of wine and liquor, some of the supplies you'll want on hand in or near your liquor cabinet include a bottle opener, bottle stoppers, cocktail napkins, cocktail shaker, corkscrew, decanter, ice bucket, pitcher, wine glasses, and shot glasses. Some wine racks have special shelves or cabinets to store these accessories.

Many companies specialize in custom-designed and ready-made wine racks and cabinets that can help you to organize all of these things. Check out these online retailers: American Wine Essentials, Inc. *(www.winecabinets.com)*, Artisans on Web *(www. aoweb.com)*, International Wine Accessories *(www. iwawine.com)*, or the Wine Enthusiast *(www.wineenthusiast.com)*.

All Clear!

Once you situate your dining room in a way that works for you and gives you a sense of having some free and open space, don't allow clutter to creep back in. It's especially tempting to let clutter build up on tabletops, particularly in an area such as the dining room if it is not used on a daily basis. Try hard not to allow your dining room table to become a drop-off spot for junk. Nothing ruins a good piece of dining room furniture as fast as the constant wear and tear of school books, pens, pots, pans, and glasses without coasters. Declare your dining room a no-clutter zone, and make sure your entire family knows it.

chapter 11

Uncluttering Your Bathrooms

WHETHER YOU HAVE PLENTY OF SPACE in your bathroom, or you're working within the confines of a tiny area, you can still organize in ways that will make your space more functional. Follow these suggestions, and you'll save yourself time and make it easier to find the things you need.

Considering Your Needs

In order to improve on your bathroom organization, first figure out what sorts of things you need to function properly within your space. You probably spend a good chunk of time each day in the bathroom shaving, doing your hair, or applying makeup, yet maybe all of the toiletry items you need are thrown in disarray under your sink cabinet. This sort of clutter wears your patience especially thin, particularly in the morning, when you're in a rush to get ready as you start your day.

When devising better ways to use your bathroom space, consider who else (your spouse, kids, teens, guests, and so on) will be using the bathroom and what their needs are. Next, evaluate what space you have available to work with by following these steps:

1. Measure your bathroom.
2. Think about how you can best work around your fixtures, including the sink, commode, shower, bathtub, medicine cabinet, mirror, towel racks, shelving, and so on.
3. Determine what you will store in the bathroom (medicines, toiletries, towels, robes, dirty laundry, reading materials, makeup, hairstyling products, and so on).

Now consider where all of these things should go, ideally, and ask yourself some more detailed questions about what you need to store in your bathroom and how you're going to store it.

- Do you have adequate shelf, closet, and cabinet space?
- Are there enough towel racks, hampers, baskets, hooks, and other organizational items in your bathroom, or do you need a better organizational system?
- Do you want to keep a magazine rack near the toilet?
- Would it be more practical to hang a hook for your robe near the bathtub?
- Do you need shelving within your shower/bathtub to store bottles of shampoo and conditioner or different types of soaps for the various people who use the bathroom?

Using Your Space to the Fullest

You don't need to do a major remodeling job to make better use of your bathroom space. Just take the time to do a thorough reorganization. Reorganizing a cluttered bathroom loaded with hairbrushes, toothpaste, Band-Aids, and other toiletries scattered everywhere can be a major task, so stay focused and tackle one bathroom at a time. Start with the bathroom that is most frequently used. Divide your bathroom into sections, including countertops, cabinets, shelves, shower, closet, and so on. Thoroughly clean and reorganize one section at a time. If you keep sight of what you need to do and what needs to go in each section, you'll be much less likely to become overwhelmed and freeze up in confusion.

Before you get started, take a look at the following list. These accessories, fixtures, and organizational tools can help you to make the most of your bathroom space. You probably won't need all of these items, so pick and choose which will be the most beneficial for you, based on your needs and the area with which you have to work.

- Clock
- Corner caddy (shelving for the bathtub/shower)
- Wall shower caddy
- Cosmetic tray
- Cotton ball/cotton swab holder
- Hair dryer
- Organizer for hair accessories
- Hamper(s)
- Liquid soap dispenser
- Magazine rack
- Over-the-commode shelves
- Radio
- Toothbrush holder
- Towel racks/towel bars (wall-mounted, over the door, or free-standing)
- Under-sink organizers (for storing cleaning supplies and other bathroom items)

Now go through each area step by step, slowly clearing out your medicine cabinet, linen closet, and other cabinets. In the medicine cabinet, for example, remove and group all of your items. Check the expiration dates and discard any old medications—these are often the biggest clutter culprits in bathrooms. No shortcuts here! When the cabinet is empty, thoroughly clean the shelves and the interior, and then return everything in an easy-to-find order. If space allows, separate each family member's prescription medications and place them on separate shelves, or at least designate certain areas on each shelf for each person. Likewise, put all of the over-the-counter medications on a separate shelf.

Bathroom Cabinets

When organizing your bathroom cabinets, also begin by taking everything out and dividing the contents into defined categories—hair care products, makeup, toiletries, prescription medications, nonprescription medications, first-aid supplies, and so on. (Keep in mind that cleaning supplies don't belong in the medicine cabinet and should be kept elsewhere, like under the kitchen sink.) As you're clearing out, make mental notes about what kind of organizational accessories might be useful.

▪ ▪ ▪ ▪ Clutter Control Quickie: Use Baskets

If you have the room, decorative baskets add a nice touch to the bathroom and also work well to store a variety of small items that need to be grouped together. Smaller baskets work well on bathroom countertops, and larger baskets with lids placed on the floor work well for storing larger items, such as hair dryers and curling irons. ▪

Store items you use every day together, such as makeup and hair care products, in areas that are easy to access. If you have a cabinet under the sink, use the back of this storage space for things you don't use every day or that are too large to fit in a medicine cabinet or on the bathroom counter.

Linen Closets

A messy linen closet is another hallmark of a die-hard clutter bug. If you're in the habit of throwing all of your towels, sheets, and other items into the closet without a second thought, complete chaos probably ensues every time you open your closet door. Maybe you don't even fold things neatly, so everything turns into a crumpled, wrinkled mess. Like every other closet or storage space in your home, you need to keep your linen closet organized, so start by unloading everything, refolding, and replacing it all in an order that makes logical sense. Arrange your towels by size, making sure that bath towels stay together, hand towels stay together, washcloths stay together, and so on.

Be sure to place the towels you're most likely to use every day front and center in your closet, and then keep less frequently used towels, such as beach or guest towels, on a less accessible shelf. Or, if you find you quickly run out of space and get the urge to start stuffing things back in, simply move the lesser-used items to another closet, such as one in a guest bedroom. Then store towels that are no longer used for personal care (but are great for bathing the dog or washing the car) out of the bathroom, with your pet or automobile supplies.

In addition to your towels, your linen closet will likely be an ideal storage place for bulky items, such as tissues, toilet paper, diapers, and storage bins filled with extra toiletry items. All of these things can be kept at the bottom of your linen closet. By organizing your closet efficiently, you might even be able to squeeze out enough extra space so that you can buy larger quantities of certain items that you use frequently. This will save you time, money, and energy, because you won't have to make as many trips to the store.

Racking Up

You might think you don't have much to work with when it comes to uncluttering your bathrooms, but there are lots of space-saving items that can make organization easier available from a variety of companies. If, for example, your bathroom lacks the necessary wall space for a towel rack near the bathtub, shower, or sink, but you don't want to deal with a jumbled heap of towels in your bathroom each day, consider purchasing an inexpensive, freestanding floor towel rack. Stacks and Stacks Home Wares *(866-376-6856, www.stacksandstacks.com)* offers an attractive three-rack free-standing towel valet (item #6880) that is narrow enough to fit even in small bathroom spaces. (Stacks and Stacks also has some unusually shaped hanging towel racks, so check them out if you do have sufficient wall space.)

▪ ▪ ▪ ▪ ▪ Clutter Control Quickie: Coping with Too Many Towels

When there are several people sharing a bathroom, towels pile up quickly—especially if you have kids. Instead of scattering towels all over the bathroom or throwing them over the bathtub and shower, save space and cut clutter by buying an inexpensive towel rack to hang on the back of your bathroom door. Then you can assign specific hooks and give different colored towels to each family member so no one gets mixed up. ▪

Restoration Hardware (800-762-1005, *www.restorationhard ware.com)* also offers a collection of highly functional bathroom organization items to help you keep mess out of your bathrooms. One of their handiest gadgets is the Hotel Wall Mount Clothes Line. Install this nine-foot retractable clothes line into your shower, and you'll never have to worry about draping wet clothes haphazardly all over the bathroom to dry again. The best part is that the sleek-looking, chrome-plated base is quite small and inconspicuous looking, and it doesn't take up any extra space.

Brookstone's Hard-to-Find Tools catalog (800-846-3000, *www.brookstone.com*) features a variety of well-made bathroom organization products. For example, the solid brass Vertical Wall Mount Bath Organizer frees up counter space by keeping bathing basics within easy reach for your morning routine. This organizer attaches to a wall and contains a cup holder, soap holder, and two swiveling towel bars. Brookstone also sells a variety of bath étagères, which easily transform wall space into valuable storage space. These units fit over most commodes and feature shelves inside polystyrene-paned doors, plus an open lower shelf. The units are made from warp-resistant wood composite materials with mildew-resistant finishes. A matching free-standing bath organizer (sold separately) offers additional storage and counter space. For redecorating your bathroom and adding functionality, Brookstone's wide selection of decorative bathroom fixtures made from solid brass, including various-sized towel bars, hooks, and towel rings, vanity shelves, showerheads, showerhead caddies, and bath tissue holders can also help you to organize the bathroom efficiently and give your bathroom a new look quickly. You'll also find similar accessories at any home improvement or hardware superstore.

Keeping Your Bathroom Clean

The bathroom is probably the toughest room in any home to keep clean and sanitary. To beat clutter for good in this high-traffic area, develop a regular cleaning routine that will help keep you mess-free once you establish your new bathroom organization.

Arm yourself with the proper tools for cleaning your bathroom, and the task will never be too daunting. Be sure to stock your arsenal with the following things:

- All-purpose cleaner
- Disinfectant
- Glass cleaner
- Mold, mildew, and soap scum remover
- Mop and bucket
- Paper towels
- Plastic bucket or organizer to hold cleaners/tools
- Plastic garbage bags
- Rubber gloves
- Broom and dustpan
- Scrubbing brush and an old toothbrush (for cleaning small, tight areas, like the crevices around your faucets)
- Soft cloths
- Sponge
- Toilet bowl brush

Make sure the upkeep doesn't get away from you by picking up bathroom clutter and quickly cleaning and disinfecting high-touch zones, such as bathroom floors, bathroom faucets, and toilet flush handles, every few days. Thoroughly clean the tub, toilet, sink/fixtures/drain, mirrors, floor, and cabinets every week. Most people dread having to scrub bathroom mold and mildew that has built up over several weeks or months, but if you keep up with this routine, the chore of cleaning the bathroom won't ever get too disgusting to deal with.

▪ ▪ ▪ ▪ ▪ Clutter Control Quickie: Fast Bathroom Cleanup

Cleaning the bathroom can be a drag, but instead of putting it off and allowing messy clutter to build, just get the job done fast. Clorox Disinfecting Wipes work wonders for quick bathroom cleaning. The 7" x 8" disposable wipes are premoistened with bleach and quickly disinfect a variety of surfaces. ▪

chapter 12

Building a Better Bedroom Environment

WHEN YOU WERE SMALL, you couldn't sleep because there were monsters under your bed. Now that you've grown up, they're still there, just in the form of *clutter* monsters under your bed—and atop your dresser, and in your closet . . . They aren't scary in the same way the bed creatures from your childhood were, but they do bring a lot of stress to your life, nonetheless. Allowing remnants of your daily routine, your work, and other aspects of your wakeful life to pile up all over your bedroom floor, explode out of your bedroom closet, or cover the surfaces of your bedroom furniture drains your energy and impedes a good night's sleep.

Scaling Back

Many people allow their bedrooms to become the drop-off spot for all sorts of stuff. When guests visit, they are less likely to see the bedroom, so why not shove all of those old magazines underneath the bed in a pinch, just to get them out of the way? For the best possible energy flow—and the best chance for peaceful, quiet personal time and restful sleep—you need a bedroom that is clutter-free. For instance, clothing retains energy from your daily life, and it should be put away. The space under your bed should be just that—space that is free and clear of too many messy boxes, books, or fuzzy bedroom slippers. Keep the knickknacks to a minimum, and remember, no snack food or dishes should be left lying around. If you keep electrical equipment such as your television, stereo, or computer in the bedroom, don't leave it running at night (noise clutter can really deter your sleep). And appliances that aren't as essential—like hair dryers, curling irons, or exercise equipment—should definitely be stored away.

▦ ▦ ▦ ▦ ▪ Clutter Control Quickie: Do Not Disturb

Privacy is essential to a cozy, uncluttered bedroom environment. If you live in a small apartment and your bedroom and living area are one in the same, it's probably difficult to keep your sleeping quarters clutter-free because of the overlap of activity. If you must sleep in a space that lacks privacy, it's best to define your sleeping area clearly and protect it from the surrounding mess with a piece of furniture, such as a bookcase or screen. ▦

In general, when cutting down on clutter in the bedroom, simply try to reduce the amount of *things* you have, from the menagerie of glass animals sitting on your shelves, to the jungle of real or artificial plants scattered all over. In fact, keeping living plants in your bedroom is actually a bad idea. At night, plants give off carbon dioxide and take in oxygen, the reverse of their daytime process.

Assessing Your Stuff

Before you get down to the nitty gritty details of organizing your bedroom, figure out exactly what you have to work with. As you've done in other instances, start by measuring the room. Then, take inventory of furniture and other large objects eating up space. Your bedroom needs the essentials—your bed, bureaus, nightstands, lamps, and so on. But what about other negotiables, like a desk, entertainment center or TV stand, exercise equipment, or full-length mirror? If your bedroom feels too cluttered, make some decisions about how much, exactly, you can afford to keep there.

Don't overcrowd your bedroom. Too many pictures on the walls, piles of books and magazines on the chairs and floor, or clothes and shoes strewn everywhere will prevent you from enjoying relaxation time in your bedroom. Even large bedrooms should be sparsely furnished. Don't feel compelled to fill every inch of space. You need room to move and breathe in your bedroom!

Eliminating clutter doesn't mean getting rid of the things you enjoy. Don't banish all the books from your bedroom, for example; just accommodate them in a way that will enhance your bedroom, rather than make it messier. Take a tip from feng shui, for instance, and try placing a pyramid-shaped bookcase in the wisdom corner of your bedroom (as you enter the room, this is the closest corner to your left). This way, books will be neatly arranged, and the shelf's pyramid shape works nicely because it is an ancient symbol of higher knowledge.

As you start clearing out your bedroom, if you realize you don't have enough of the right items to help you stay organized, consider the approximate size of each new item you're thinking about adding, determine how it will be used, and where it will go. You might need a new trunk to store all of those sweaters that end up in a lump at the bottom of your closet, but there's no use running out and buying one unless you're sure it will fit.

■ ■ ■ ■ Clutter Control Quickie: Don't Mix Work and Sleep

If possible, keep your work area in another room, or at least put it away or cover it up when you turn in at night. Work and sleep just don't mix. Your brain is cluttered enough during the day with thoughts of balancing your work and home life—the last thing you need is to drift off to sleep surrounded by reminders of that stress. And you don't want any of that work-related para-phernalia to prompt a frustrating dream about the office! ■

By this point, if you've already tackled your closets (and you should have, unless you cheated and skipped Chapter 7), you're a step ahead of the game, because you've most likely sorted through your hanging wardrobe. If you've cut any corners in this department, now is the time to figure out which items actually belong in your bedroom closet and which can be stored elsewhere. Can winter jackets be stored in a foyer closet or in the basement, attic, or garage during the off-season? What about personal items, such as framed photographs and other belongings? If, for instance, the tops of your dressers are overly crowded with all of these personal tidbits, you need shelves or some other type of wall space to accommodate that extra stuff.

Carefully analyze each item in your bedroom and determine whether it's being used to its maximum potential. Could you better utilize your dresser drawer space if you reorganized them? If you were to store your sweaters and/or linens in a container under your bed, could you free up valuable closet space? If you installed a shoe rack in your closet, could you cut clutter with a better organized shoe collection?

If certain things in your bedroom only take up space, it's probably time to get rid of them—or at least store them someplace out of the way. You know you've got critical clutter issues in your bedroom when, for example, you have a treadmill or exercise bike, and the only purpose it serves is as a place to pile laundry or a spot to hang your bath towel after you shower! Free up the space completely or replace it with something smaller and more functional that provides better storage space.

If you understand what your needs are and evaluate all of the space available in your bedroom, you'll be able to choose which pieces of furniture and which types of storage solutions will provide the most functionality and comfort.

Blending Aesthetics with Function

Clearing out clutter from your bedroom is all well and good, but no one wants to scale back to the point of creating a space devoid of personality. Part of what makes a bedroom feel comfortable and lived-in are the extra, individualized touches you give it. When you're ready to turn your focus to the décor of your bedroom, consider which personal touches work best in your bedroom, including photographs, artwork, trinkets, silk flowers, and so on. Be selective about which items you decide to keep in your bedroom, and think about functionality as well as visual appeal.

Try not to overload a small piece of furniture with excess inessentials. With your nightstand, for instance, determine which essentials—alarm clock, books, telephone, lamp, reading glasses, TV remote control, and so on—are necessary. Remember, your nightstand is not a final destination for leftover food, empty drinking glasses, and so on. If you're in the habit of leaving other personal items atop your nightstand, such as your keys, wallet, watch, or whatever else, invest in a nightstand with a drawer, so you can store excess clutter neatly away at night.

As you did in your living area, consider the placement of your bedroom furniture in light of the location of your electrical outlets, light switches, cable TV jacks, and phone jacks. Save yourself from wire clutter and avoid running unsightly, potentially dangerous extension cords across the room.

Tackling Those Dreaded Dresser Drawers

Well-organized dressers are essential for storing wardrobe items that don't fit in your closet. When organizing your dresser, remove everything from the drawers and lay the items on a bed or the floor. Take careful inventory and determine what needs to be kept in the dresser. It's easy for a clutter bug to stick all sorts of miscellaneous, unrelated items, such as birthday cards or prescription instructions, into dresser drawers just to keep them out of the way, but these only take up valuable space, contribute to the wrinkling of your clothes, and add to your clutter problem. Remember those plastic storage containers that just solved your linen storage problems? Go out and grab some smaller styles, designate separate containers for different items, and stack them neatly in an out-of-the-way spot, like the top of a closet shelf. Then, every time you get a special card or letter you want to save, you can immediately place it in its proper container.

▓ ▓ ▓ ▓ ■ Clutter Control Quickie: Box Them Up

To end clutter in your dresser drawers, insert one or two shoeboxes or small containers to keep socks, pantyhose, or other small items separate. If your drawers are too small to accommodate those containers, use resealable storage bags instead. This way, these things won't spill over onto other clothes in your drawers. ▓

After you clear out all your drawers, the next step is to group all similar items together, either by season or clothing type. Consider the number of drawers your dresser has, and determine where each group of items should be stored. Store items you use everyday, such as socks, pantyhose, and underwear, in the drawer that's the most convenient to access. Once you set up this system, don't slip. Remember to keep T-shirts in one drawer, underwear in the other, and so forth.

If two people are sharing a dresser, each person should have his or her own drawers, to maintain better organization. In order to maximize space, fold all of your laundry neatly, don't just stuff it into the drawers. Unfolded laundry doesn't just make for more wrinkles, it takes up extra space, exacerbating clutter.

Lots of people choose to store their jewelry in a dresser drawer, and that's fine, as long as you keep it organized. Place the pieces into divided containers in a particular drawer. It might also make sense to keep your most frequently used jewelry on a jewelry holder or in a jewelry box, for easier access.

▓ ▓ ▓ ▓ ■ Clutter Control Quickie: Jewelry Storage Shortcuts

Instead of using an expensive jewelry box that takes up lots of room, consider using plastic ice cube trays or foam egg cartons to store your jewelry in a dresser drawer. This works great with earrings, rings, pins, bracelets, and some necklaces, and it costs next to nothing! ▓

Conquering Clutter Monsters Under the Bed

Although it's tempting, never throw random things under the bed. Yes, this area is great for storage, but it's useless if it's a disorganized mess. Devise ways to store items properly before putting anything under the bed. Then, resist the urge to shove anything and everything underneath when you're in a rush to clean up. Declare the area beneath your bed a junk-free zone and you'll boost your clutter control potential tremendously.

Underbed storage is an ideal place to keep off-season clothing, bedding, and other bulky items. Manage this valuable space properly with airtight plastic bins or hide-away drawers. Stacks and Stacks (866-376-6856, *www.stacksandstacks.com*) offers a large selection of storage solutions for use under a bed, including a unit that fits most twin through king-sized beds with metal frames.

▨ ▨ ▨ ▨ ▨ Clutter Control Quickie: Mind Your Mattress Measurements

Thinking about purchasing a new bed? You need to be aware of more than merely the dimensions of the mattress. When determining whether a bed will fit in your room, remember to leave at least 15" on either side so you have ample area to move around. This will help you to feel less cluttered in your bedroom space. ▨

Stacks and Stacks also markets an underbed cedar storage container. This wooden chest is ideal for shoes, sweaters, and year-round storage, and it really maximizes unused space beneath the bed. The unit features a hardboard bottom and sliding top that have an easy-to-clean lacquer finish. Removable casters allow units to be stacked.

Airtight plastic containers (with wheels) designed specifically to be stored under a bed are another alternative. These transparent plastic containers, available at most mass-market retailers, allow you to see what's inside easily. And because they're on wheels, they can be pulled out from under the bed with ease.

Storing Sheets and Other Bedding Accessories

Bedding items take up lots of storage space. For each bed in your house, you need at least a few sets of sheets, plus blankets, bedspreads, or comforters, and all that bulk adds up. If your linens are poorly organized, things can get untidy. As you're uncluttering your bedroom, determine what your exact needs are for each bed in your home and whether or not the storage system you have at present for your linens is working.

To keep your bedding organized, maintain an inventory of three complete linen sets. This way, one set can always be kept on the bed (in use), one can be in the laundry, and one can be in storage. Rotate the three sets regularly. When bed linens aren't actually in use on a bed, store them properly. If your linen closet is stuffed to the gills, cut out that clutter. It's difficult to find what you need when sheets are packed in every which way, and it's damaging to the fabric. Instead, store your linens neatly, somewhere out of the way. Linens should always be laundered before being stored. Keep sheets and pillowcases in plastic bags in a cool and dry spot, out of direct light. Linens should always be stored in a way that protects them from moisture, to keep them free from mold and mildew. Storing the items in a plastic bag also ensures against damage from moths or other insects. Large plastic storage containers, such as those described in the previous section, are great for storing extra linens once you properly pack them in plastic.

▨ ▨ ▨ ▨ ▨ Clutter Control Quickie: Keep Plastic Sheet Packages

When purchasing a new package of sheets, think twice before tossing the plastic packaging. Higher quality sheets are often sold in resealable plastic pouches that can be used for storage during the life of the item. These will come in handy if you decide to free up space in closets by packing away your sheets. ▨

Storing your comforters and blankets is another smart way to cut clutter from your bedroom and make way for items you need to keep readily available for use every day. Always launder or dry-clean them first. Because blankets and comforters can be compressed easily, it's tempting to squash them down in storage to save space. Don't overfold or crush a down comforter or pillow, however. Allow it to remain as fluffy as possible. Loosely wrap the comforter or blanket in plastic, and then store it in a cool, dry place, such as a closet, wooden (cedar) storage chest, dresser drawer (if the drawer is large enough), or in an airtight plastic container. Fold blankets, put them in a cotton pillowcase, and then place them in a closet. (Remember to keep blankets and comforters out of direct sunlight when storing them, to avoid fading.)

■ ■ ■ ■ **Clutter Control Quickie: Fill Your Pillowcases**

Save yourself from having to rifle through your linen closet in search of the matching components of a complete sheet set. Store each set inside its matching pillowcase, then fold the open end of the pillowcase around the sheets and stack each set in your linen closet. This way, everything you need will always be stored neatly together. ■

Nothing adds to the mess and clutter of a bedroom like an unmade bed with blankets and comforters left around on the floor. If you have some extra space in your bedroom, blankets and comforters that aren't in use can also be stored using a free-standing blanket or quilt rack. These are typically made of wood and should be placed near the foot of a bed. This type of rack can add to the décor of a room and is a stand-alone piece of furniture that doubles as a storage solution.

Considering Your Guest Room

In most people's homes, space is tight. If you've designated a room to be your guest room, but you don't have guests often, you probably use this space for other activities as well. Maybe you use your guest room as an exercise room, as space for a certain hobby, a room to display your knickknacks or collections, a reading room, or a home office.

When guests do use this room, make sure it's not so cluttered that it prevents them from having a comfortable stay in your home. Organize a storage space with all of the essentials guests need in one spot. This includes a complete bed linen set, two pillows, extra blankets, towels, and toiletries (especially soap and shampoo). If closet space is tight, invest in a lightweight, freestanding cart with drawers to hold these essentials. Be sure that the room allows for a space where guests can store luggage and perhaps unpack into a few empty dresser drawers. At the very least, provide space for the guest to hang up garments in a closet, or purchase a freestanding clothing rack from any hardware store or mass-market retailer. As with all of the rooms in your home, take advantage of organizational products, like specialty hangers, underbed storage bins, dresser drawers, and shelving to organize and properly store belongings in your guest room.

If you really want to set up a separate guest room area in your home, but don't feel you have enough space to fit a full-sized traditional bed, consider some of the following alternatives.

Air Mattress

The AeroBed (*www.aerobed.com*) self-inflates fully in less than a minute and deflates in just fifteen seconds. It has a powerful built-in electric pump for fast, easy inflation. Just plug it in, touch a button, and the AeroBed inflates into a thick and comfortable mattress. AeroBed is inexpensive, comes in several popular bed sizes, and uses standard size sheets. When not in use, it deflates to the size of a sleeping bag, making it extremely easy to store in a closet.

Futon

The biggest benefit to futons is that they're more affordable than sofa beds. And, when not used as a bed, a futon can also be used as a couch. Unless you purchase a high-end futon, however, these are often uncomfortable, and they take up the same amount of space as a full-sized couch or sofa bed.

Sofa Bed

When not used as a bed, these double as full-sized couches that come in a wide range of styles. Typically queen or king size, some sofa beds also have custom-size mattresses. The cost for sofa beds varies greatly, based on the quality of the couch as well as the type and quality of the mattress built into it. Some sofa beds can be uncomfortable to sit and sleep on.

Portable Cot

These metal frames on wheels fold in half for easy storage in a basement and utilize a thin (often foam) mattress. They come in several different sizes and tend to be extremely inexpensive. Most people, however, don't find them very comfortable.

Wall Bed

If you're building a home office and want it to double as a comfortable guest room, Techline *(www.techlineusa.com)* offers a stylish, well-constructed home office furniture system that includes a pull-down wall bed. This system allows you to utilize the room space available to include a full-sized desk, shelves, cabinets, plus the pull-down bed that sets up in minutes.

■ ■ ■ ■ ■ Clutter Control Quickie: Set the Right Mood

First and foremost, your bedroom is a place to rest your body, mind, and spirit. Be mindful of your decorative elements and their sensory impact. Rather than cluttering your bedroom with unnecessary junk, surround yourself with calm colors, soothing fabrics, relaxing music, aromatic candles, and subdued lighting to help you release the stresses of your day and prepare you for a restful night's sleep. ■

chapter 13

Controlling Clutter with Your Kids

ARE YOUR KIDS' BEDROOMS complete disaster areas? Is the playroom such a mess it looks like a bomb exploded in Toyland? Whether or not you mean for it to happen, toy and clothing pileup can quickly engulf your kids' rooms. And just as clutter impedes your life, it will make it harder for your kids to function properly as well.

The main problem with kids' space is simply an overabundance of stuff. Often, well-meaning parents load their kids down with way too many clothes, shoes, toys, and electronic gadgets—all the things parents think children should have in order to have a fantastic childhood. There's nothing inherently wrong with any of these things, it's just that many times, it all gets to be too much.

One sure sign of stuff run amok is a telltale mountain of clothes piled atop the dresser, as your child stands before it, unable to decide what to wear. When your child crankily declares, "I don't have anything to wear," what she really means is, "I have too many things to choose from and can't make a decision!" The same holds true with that mound of toys—or whatever else there's too much of in your kids' rooms. Having too many options is cumbersome, especially to younger children who just aren't equipped to deal with those kinds of choices yet.

All of this excess stuff takes up valuable space in closets, dressers, and other storage spaces, until it begins to overflow and spawn monster piles everywhere. If you or your kids have too much stuff, inevitably some of it will never be used to the best advantage, because it's just too difficult to deal with, and this does no one any good.

▧ ▧ ▧ ▧ ▧ Clutter Control Quickie: Eliminate Inessentials

The best way to stay on top of kid clutter is getting rid of anything that's not absolutely necessary. If you buy a month's supply of diapers to save money, don't store them in the middle of the nursery where they'll clutter up valuable space. Discard toys that are broken or that your children have outgrown. Also, clean out drawers and closet space frequently so they aren't cluttered with clothing that no longer fits or that your kids no longer wear. ▧

Evaluating Your Options

If the above scenario reminds you of your own family's situation, it's time to get down to serious organizational business where the kids are concerned. Begin the process of organizing your kids' rooms by asking yourself the following questions:

- How much space is available? (Measure the room carefully.)
- How old is your child and what are his or her primary needs in the bedroom?
- Is this an area where your child spends a lot of free time playing or studying?
- What are your child's special interests? How can these interests be accommodated within the room?
- Do your kids have their own rooms, or do they share space? (Clutter control is even tougher when two children share a room. You also have to consider privacy issues.)
- Is excess electrical equipment—computer, TV, stereo, telephone—cluttering up space in your kids' rooms?
- Is the closet space in your kids' rooms being used to best advantage?
- Is there adequate space to store toys, equipment for sports and other hobbies, collections, and so on? Or, do

you need to invest in different sorts of toy chests, book-cases, dressers, and shelving to reduce clutter?

- Does the furniture that is currently in your kids' rooms help you in your clutter control crusade, or does it make life harder? For instance, if the room is too small to accommodate two stand-alone twin beds, would it make more sense to switch to bunk beds?

Motivating Your Kids

Now that you know what you've got to work with and what things you need to focus on to control clutter in your kids' rooms, you need to motivate your kids to jump onto the cleanup bandwagon. Okay, maybe *kids* and *cleanup* seem like mutually exclusive terms. But cleaner, neater kids' play areas and bedrooms *can* be achieved by using some smart psychology.

1. In a friendly, congenial way, ask your child if he or she would like some help putting things away. Sometimes, children—especially younger children—are reluctant to work alone because the task seems overwhelming. But if you pitch in, even a little bit, a child's enthusiasm often grows. Just be sure you're not the one doing all the work. If you want your kids to learn good clutter control skills, the lion's share of the cleanup should be theirs!

2. If you don't think your child uses or plays with certain items anymore, don't just start putting them away or, worse, threatening to throw them out. Like anyone else, kids are fiercely protective of their things. Respect your child's need for privacy and ownership.

3. Ask your kids if they still *really* enjoy playing with certain toys or if particular items hold a special meaning for them. If not, suggest donating those things to children who really will enjoy using them. Children are often happy to know

they can help other kids who are less fortunate, so this can be a great motivator. Make sure, of course, that any items you donate have all their parts and are in good, working condition. You don't want to give your children the mistaken impression that it's all right to pass on unusable junk to charity.

4. Create opportunities for storage solutions by placing "collection containers" in your kids' playroom and bedrooms. If there is a designated place for catching clutter, then it will become part of a more organized thought process—the first step toward elimination! Hampers and colorful toy boxes with safety lids work well. Just make sure they can't shut on a child if he should try to hide inside them.

5. Take the lead by becoming a positive example to your children. If you clear your own clutter, you might inspire your children to do the same!

However you decide to tackle clutter control with your kids, be creative and have fun. That's the surest way to capture your kids' interest and attention.

Kid Clutter Basics

When handling clutter control with your kids, begin by making sure the bedroom is used for its rightful purpose and that the potential for properly learning, relaxing, and sleeping is maximized. For starters, take all of the loose stuff hanging out around the room and designate some appropriate homes. Group and shelve all of the books according to whether they are for learning, or for fun. Once you start to organize your kids' stuff in this way, you might notice that they instantly become more interested in learning, because the room's atmosphere is more conducive to concentration.

Computers, Videos, and Electronics

We've already seen that it's a good idea to keep work/office-related clutter out of your bedroom and living areas, but it's especially important when kids are involved. If at all possible, keep the computers, TVs, and video games out of the your children's bedrooms. Imagine an eight-year-old who just can't fall asleep at night. Now picture this child's room full of all sorts of stuff—DVDs stacked up next to a TV/VCR unit, a video game system with a jumble of cartridges, a computer, and all sorts of other electronic equipment. In the midst of this electronic playground, there are scads of books, toys, and clothes piled everywhere. It's no wonder the child can't unwind at bedtime! Remember, kids' bedrooms are for sleeping, relaxing, and studying—not for watching all-night TV when they should be drifting off to dreamland.

Too much disorganized stuff in the bedroom is just as distracting to your kids as it is to you—it breeds mental clutter and breaks concentration. Remember, it is your job as a parent to teach your children how to create spaces that will serve the proper purpose and most benefit their growth.

▒ ■ ■ ■ ■ Clutter Control Quickie: Set for Sleep Time

With kids, maintaining clutter control is important for setting the right atmosphere at bedtime. In order to sleep in peace, your kids need a peaceful room—that means no X-Men wielding their super powers, no Power Puff Girls punching people out, and definitely no play guns hanging around. Keep those kinds of toys stored away at night so that their negative energy won't interfere with your children's study or sleep time. ■

Saving Your "Wreck" Room

In your house, do you have a rec room, or a "wreck room," that's disorganized and full of clutter? You've probably tried hard to create an exciting life for your kids, so the playroom is full of all sorts of stuff. In essence, however, the amount of *stuff* that has accumulated could be causing unnecessary clutter and actually blocking your kids' creativity and energy.

Your rec room should not become a dumping ground for all the toys in the house. Nor should it be completely spare. A good balance in this room should include a *small* variety of stimulating toys, books, games, and videos to help your children have fun and expand their minds.

▪ ▪ ▪ ▪ ▪ Clutter Control Quickie: Compartmentalize the Toy Box

If you really want to step up clutter control with your kids, use plastic bins or shoe boxes to separate toys with lots of small pieces for more organized storage in the toy box. This strategy works well with building blocks, toy cars, board games, action figures, dolls (and their accessories), and trading cards. ▪

If you have too much clutter in your rec room, donate some of it to your doctor's office for their waiting room or to a battered women's shelter, where kids often stay as well. Put extra items to a healthier use in another space, and keep space for your kids' play area as open and inviting as possible.

Hitting the Books

Sure, creating a productive study area for your kids is about making the best possible use of space and keeping the desktop clear of unnecessary junk, but there's more to it than this. For starters, consider the furniture. Position the desk so that your children are angled toward and facing the doorway rather than with their backs to it, so they can see what's going on. If you can't position the desk any other way and the child's back is to the door, hang a mirror so that the child can see things in the reflection. With their backs facing the door, children might feel as if people or things can sneak up on them, and they might not be able to concentrate.

The desk chair needs to be free and clear to move, so that

means no excess stuff piling up on the floor around it. Also watch out for unnecessary visual clutter in the form of posters, pictures, or book covers with angry or hostile scenes—these can cause study disturbances. Instead, position a few pictures that symbolize higher aspirations, such as mountain scenes. Also, don't face your kids' desks toward a window, since all the out-side activity they can see will diminish their attention span.

▨ ▨ ▨ ▨ ▨ Clutter Control Quickie: Smart Storage for Kids

Since stuff under the bed can scare younger children and lead to sleep distur-bances, it's best to store extra toys, books, and clothing neatly in boxes you can stack in a closet. Make sure you keep the storage boxes within safe reach for kids, and make them partners in keeping the toys where they belong by scheduling a nightly toy cleanup. ▨

Ideally, your child should be able to study in one room and sleep in another. This is not always practical, so when study time has to be conducted in the bedroom, be sure to wrap things up properly when it's time to close the books and go to bed. Keep your children's morning routines free of clutter by having them place their books in their book bag for school the next day and clear off their desks every night before turning out the lights. This will bring closure to the day's work and make you both feel ready and able to tackle a new day.

Finding Solutions When Space Is Tight

Struggling to control clutter in limited space is always tough, but it is, perhaps, toughest when trying to organize a functional bed-room for a child. Children have ever-growing toy collections, not to mention an ever-changing wardrobe and an abundance of other toys and equipment that they need to store.

It's ideal if, as your kids get older, they can have their own rooms. Especially if kids are more than a few years apart, sharing rooms can be tough. Kids need their own privacy and adequate space to play and express themselves. When kids are sharing tight bedroom quarters, there's much more of a chance that things won't run smoothly and clutter will pile up.

If your kids need to share a room, make sure they both have adequate and equal space, or there will be lots of arguments. Each child needs to have something in the room that is uniquely his or hers in order to feel as if the space belongs to them. To better cope with kids living in tight quarters, consider these options to maximize the space you do have (see subsequent sections in this chapter for more details on some of these options):

- Add hooks on the closet door(s) and inside the closet (on the side walls) for jackets, shoe bags, and other items.
- Free up floor space by utilizing a loft bed for your child. The sleeping area can be on top, while a desk, dresser, shelves, or other storage space can be built beneath the bed.
- Whenever possible, choose pieces of furniture designed with multiple uses in mind. For example, some children's beds already have shelving or drawers built in.
- Make full use of closet organization tools (described in Chapter 7) to maximize every inch of available closet space.
- Invest in a toy chest that is large enough to function as a primary holding spot for the majority of your kids' toys.
- Install shelving on the walls as opposed to using a free-standing shelf unit that would take up floor space. These are great for storing books, toys, collectibles, trophies, and other items.
- Display shelving, which you can install about a foot down from the ceiling, is great for items your kids want to keep in view but don't necessarily need to use every day. Use these for collections, trophies, and artwork.

Clutter Control as Kids Grow

When kids are little, toys, games, and stuffed animals need putting away; as they get older, the clutter morphs into clothes, CDs, and electronics that overtake the space. Children's rooms should always be kept free of clutter. If you make clutter cleanup fun from the time they are young by using imaginative toy boxes, clothing hooks, and other creative, whimsical organizers, your kids might actually want to keep things neat on their own as they grow—or at least be a little less averse to the idea.

Keeping a Baby's Room Simple

It is not uncommon for parents—especially first-time parents—to overdecorate their new baby's bedroom. Preparing for baby's arrival is fun and exciting, but don't overdo it or concern yourself too much with interior design trends. For infants and small children, simplicity is key. Avoid hanging too many mobiles or other toys from the ceiling. One or two gentle mobiles will do it. Also, don't clutter a baby's crib with too many toys. It's best to have interesting textures and toys on the floor, for children to explore them when they are awake.

■ ■ ■ ■ ■ Clutter Control Quickie: Use the Right Changing Table

It's a long road to toilet training a toddler, and you're going to be changing a lot of diapers along the way. If you're expecting a new baby, invest in a changing table with drawers and/or shelves beneath it so wipes, creams, and diapers are within arm's reach for you, but not for your baby. This will help you to organize everything you need, while keeping things out of your baby's range. ■

Don't clutter your baby's senses with an onslaught of bright color in the nursery. Muted colors, especially pastels and warm, gentle earth tones, as well as soft textures in bedding and furnishings, are best for encouraging a restful state. Once your child wakes up, she can experience intense colors and textures throughout the rest of the house, but her bedroom should be as quiet, peaceful, and calm as possible.

As your child grows from an infant to a toddler, floor space will become increasingly important, because this is where your child will play. Try to maximize floor space as much as possible. To generate more floor space, utilize lighting that attaches to the ceiling or walls (as opposed to floor lamps) and take advantage of vertical storage spaces (tall bookcases or dressers with more drawers stacked vertically as opposed to being wide).

Wherever possible, store larger toys and accessories (such as rockers, walkers, bouncers, swings, and so on) in closets when they're not in use. A toy bin is ideal for small to mid-sized toys, while shelves or a basket (placed in the floor or on a dresser) can be used to display teddy bears and other stuffed toys in a decorative manner. Remember to make the effort to keep toy chests organized—don't just toss toys in.

▪ ▪ ▪ ▪ Clutter Control Quickie: Double Up

Because young children change and grow so quickly, it's good to arm yourself with tools that serve more than one purpose when fighting kids' clutter. The Everything 4 Baby Web site *(http://everything4baby.freeyellow.com)* offers a hand-woven, elephant-shaped hamper made from durable wicker that can double as a storage box for toys as your child gets older. ▪

Cutting Through Older Kids' Messes

The process of organizing your preteen or teen's room is much the same as it is when organizing your own master bedroom (see Chapter 12). Except kids grow and change so quickly that you might need to reevaluate things more frequently. As your child gets older, his or her needs will change dramatically, so it is important to reassess their bedroom situation. Storage space becomes more of a premium, and issues such as privacy become increasingly more important.

▓ ▓ ▓ ▓ ■ Clutter Control Quickie: End-of-School Cleanup

Kids acquire quite a bit of clutter through the course of each school year. Naturally, you'll want to save special pictures or papers, but if you hold on to every single thing, the clutter will consume you! At the end of each school year, go through your child's bookshelves and piles of papers to determine what you can get rid of, or if you can store old textbooks and papers to make room for next year's things. ▓

Periodically retake inventory of your kids' furniture to be sure it still suits their needs. The right furniture will help to keep your kids' rooms on the right track. Furnishings should be sized appropriately for children, and it's especially useful if pieces can be augmented or replaced as they grow. If you need to purchase new bedroom furniture as your children grow, consider the size of each piece and determine exactly how it will be used and where in the room it will go.

Also sort through everything stored in their bedrooms regularly, including his or her wardrobe (twice a year is ideal). Just as you did with your own dresser, have your teen remove everything, take careful inventory, determine what needs to be kept in the dresser, and group similar items together. As you've done with your own room, figure out which items actually belong in the bedroom and what can be stored elsewhere.

Finding the Right Furniture

The furniture in your kids' rooms should maximize storage space. For example, a loft bed (with a desk or dresser below it) will save space and make the most out of a small area because the wall space (in addition to floor space) is being utilized.

Bunksnstuff.com (800-355-1997, *www.bunksnstuff.com*) is just one online furniture source specializing in space-saving bunk beds and loft beds that are great for a child or teen's bedroom. The company's bunk/loft system offers a complete bedroom set in one unit. The set includes two twin beds, as well as a built-in three-drawer desk, two-shelf bookcase, and a 22" deep five-drawer chest. The desk and bookshelves can be placed on either side and are reversible.

If you're in search of a single twin-size bed with plenty of drawer storage below it, Bunks 'n' Stuff offers what it calls the Captain's Bed. This standard twin bed has an oversized center drawer that can be used for anything from a toy chest to a file cabinet. A matching dresser, desk, and nightstand are also available.

Bunk Beds Plus (219-672-3491, *www.bunkbedsplus.com*), Bhome.com (800-288-7632, *www.behome.com*), and the Great American Bunk Bed Company (866-4US-BUNK, *www.great americanbunkbed.com*) are other good online retailers of bunk beds and storage solutions for a child's bedroom.

The potential for extra storage is a key consideration when purchasing bunk beds, but don't forget to consider safety guidelines as well:

- The bed should be made of strong, durable materials with edges that are smooth and rounded. After the unit is installed, shake the bed vigorously to be sure it's firm and stable.
- The guardrails should run the length of the bed on both sides of the upper bunk.
- The ladder should be wide, securely attached, and at a comfortable climbing angle.
- The mattress used with the bed should be the proper size and have a snug fit (some bunk beds utilize custom-sized mattresses). The mattress should be supported by strong slats that are tightly screwed into the side of the bed.

As previously mentioned, younger children often don't like stuff stored under their beds, but that doesn't mean you shouldn't take full advantage of underbed storage where older kids are concerned. Also consider using closet organizers to utilize closet space fully. Think carefully about what the room is being used for and plan accordingly. If your child will be doing homework, practicing an instrument, or using a computer, create a quiet, uncluttered environment that is conducive. Because most teens have an abundance of electronic equipment (computer, TV, VCR, DVD player, video game system, alarm clock, stereo, telephone, and so on), make sure the room has ample electrical outlets and that these outlets are in locations where extension cords won't have to be overused.

To help your preteen or teen keep his or her room organized, create an environment where everything has its proper place. Then, it'll just be a matter of convincing your teen to put his or her belongings back. If a teen is given the opportunity to pile up dirty laundry in the middle of the bedroom, that's what will happen unless you provide a convenient hamper or laundry basket. Likewise, less trash will end up on the floor if a good-sized wastebasket is placed in the room and is easily accessible.

■ ■ ■ ■ ■ Clutter Control Quickie: Set Toy Limits

A good way to stay on top of kid clutter is to limit the number of toys you allow your children to leave out at one time. Make a rule that any toy that isn't being actively used be put away before a new toy can be taken out. For an infant or toddler, keep only a few toys out in the open and rotate them every few days. Promptly throw out broken toys and give away those that your kids no longer play with. ■

In general, children's rooms need to change and grow as they do. Children should be given the deciding vote in how their room will look. Allow your children some freedom in accessorizing their bed linens, toys and toy containers, wall decorations, and even some of their furnishings, and they will be more inspired and enthusiastic about controlling their own clutter.

Rearranging or changing furnishings and varying décor are important as their needs change. A little bit of autonomy will go a long way toward teaching children to make decisions and build strong organizational skills. Remember, keep things simple, cut out the clutter, and you'll be on your way to creating a better space for your kids.

Once you whip the kids' rooms into shape, be sure to do regular space cleanings to keep those clutter monsters away! If you stay on top of the clutter on a daily basis, it will be much less likely to creep back up on you.

chapter 14

Maintaining a Work Space That Works for You

IF YOUR OFFICE IS A TOTAL DISASTER AREA, with papers piled high, files flung everywhere, and sticky notes, staples, pens, and paperclips galore, you need to get your act together. But where do you even start, when there's not a single inch of uncluttered desk space to be seen? Whether you believe it or not, it's actually easier to get a handle on clutter in your office, because your work environment is more structured than other areas of your life. At home, you have full reign to do as you please. The more options you have, the more involved the decision-making process becomes. At work, however, there are fewer options. You have particular assignments to complete, responsibilities to fulfill, and resources available to you. You work within the confines of your job duties, and, in a sense, it becomes easier to work within these set limitations.

Stress-Proofing Your Work Life

Work can be rewarding, but it can also be a major source of stress. If certain aspects of your work are more stressful than you can comfortably handle, take steps to get your job stress under control. Remember, some stress can be good. It can get you motivated and boost your performance. You just don't want to exceed your stress tolerance level—at least not too often.

Before you attempt to unclutter your physical work space, think about what's contributing to your mental clutter at work. Consider how you feel about the people you work with, your supervisors, and your work environment. Also think about the specific work you do day-to-day: Do you feel it's important? Does the job suit your skills, challenge you, and meet your needs? What are your favorite—and least favorite—parts of the job? Do you feel as if you generally have enough time to accomplish what needs to be done at work, or are you always scrambling to catch up? How would you change your job, if you could? Writing about these things might help you to understand what's contributing to your crazed work environment.

▪ ▪ ▪ ▪ ▪ Clutter Control Quickie: Avoid Interruptions

Throughout the work day, especially when you're trying to focus on accomplishing a specific task, keep interruptions to a minimum. Each time you get interrupted, it breeds mental clutter. Not only are you kept from completing the task you're working on, you're also distracted, causing you to spend extra time refocusing after the interruption. ▪

What if you enjoy the work itself, but your hectic schedule and surroundings are driving you crazy? Without a conducive work environment, your attitude on the job—and your job performance—will suffer. If you know you need an attitude adjustment at work, reflect on what's important to you and what you need to create a better work experience. Keep in mind that your priorities might not always mesh with those of your bosses or colleagues. Maybe, for instance, the people you work with are gung ho to get a huge project done by the end of the day, yet you've barely had a moment to catch your breath after finishing your last project. Don't let this rattle you. Naturally, you need to get your projects done, but if you know you need to take a little time to get your bearings and reorganize before you blindly leap into the next task, trust your instincts.

Maybe you don't believe you have the time at work to reconfigure your space or reassess your game plan, but solid organization will have a significant impact on the quality of the work you do. For starters, simply keeping things in their appropriate place and making sure they are easily accessible will help you to work more efficiently. Arranging your space to fit your needs and comforts will have a tremendous influence on your stress level, motivation, and self-esteem as well.

The first step to uncluttering your office space is setting up an ordered system so you know exactly where to find anything easily. Don't worry; your system doesn't have to be elaborate. It just has to make sense to you. The more familiar the system, the easier it will be to stick with it.

■ ■ ■ ■ ■ Clutter Control Quickie: Grab a Helping Hand

Learning to delegate responsibility can free up your time and reduce work that your particular skills, experience, and knowledge aren't required for. At work, subordinates can be assigned to gather facts, prepare rough drafts of letters and reports, sort through mail, make photocopies or handle printing and collating. Delegating responsibility will help reduce your stress level and free up your time so that you can concentrate on more important things. ■

Most offices are filled with the standard, garden variety filing cabinets, paper trays, and bulletin or dry erase boards, but there are lots of other options that can help you to get a better handle on your work space. By making your office your own, you'll be more motivated and inspired while at your desk. Add some personal touches, and your work space won't seem so dull and it won't drag you down. Here are some simple ideas to start you on the path to office clutter control.

- Add a shelf or small bookcase that will allow you to access the things you need more easily. These will also give your space a more sophisticated feel.
- Get a few desktop organizers for common supplies such as pens, paper clips, staplers, staples, sticky notes, scissors, and calculators.
- Find some small, matching storage units for computer disks, CDs, message slips, phone numbers, and other basic odds and ends.

- Make room under your desk for a small cart of drawers—you'll have more space to work if you get all that clutter off your desk!

Pounce on the Paper Problem

Just like at home, your organizational efforts at work will go far if you immediately tackle the king of all clutter: paper. As thin as a single sheet is, paper has a tendency to multiply and accumulate at an amazing rate. In fact, it's probably taking up more room than you even realize right now.

Paper not only clutters your desk, it also takes over your ability to prioritize and get things done. It's a problem that just keeps coming back for more. Once you have it, it is hard to get rid of, and if you waste your time rifling through the same piles of disorganized paper over and over, it becomes a strain on your productivity.

▨ ▨ ▨ ▨ ▨ Clutter Control Quickie: Avoid Overextension

Studies show that most highly productive managers in the workplace have learned to take on only about three major tasks or priorities each day. By spending time focusing on just a few important tasks (plus a few less important obligations or unexpected details that creep up), you can better direct your attention and devote adequate time to accomplishing what needs to get done. ▨

Take a look at the current paper situation in your office. Do you already have a system in the works, but you just don't keep up with it? Or maybe you've never even considered a system. Whatever the case, this is the time to get it under control. Once you have the paper problem by the throat, the rest of the fire can be extinguished rather easily.

Most of the paper you encounter during a work day needs to be handled only once. Say, for instance, you receive a memo informing you of a company meeting in a week. You probably look at the memo and then put it aside for later. Now there's a good chance that this one little piece of paper will be swallowed by the stack of other vagrant papers on your desk, never to be seen again.

Until a week later, that is, when the meeting finally rolls around and you reach for the piles of paper strewn everywhere on your desk in order to locate the missing information. Yes, it is in there, but finding it is a different story. Now you're handling the same papers you've handled a thousand times before, to no avail. You've already wasted time and energy wracking your brain to remember where you put that lost piece of paper, then sorting through the stack, yet failing to find it.

You could have saved yourself a lot of frustration if, upon first receiving the memo, you simply entered the appointment in your planner and threw the piece of paper away! When it comes to paper, try to apply the "handle only once" rule as often as you can. If you do this, you'll be surprised at what an impact paper management has on clutter control.

File Away!

If you can't throw something away, don't leave it lying around! As soon as you're finished with a piece of paper, figure out what needs to be done with it and put it in its appropriate place. This is where an organized filing system comes into play. Most people arrange files alphabetically because it's convenient and simple. If you really want to get serious, find another way to further organize your files, such as numerically, by date, geographically, by subject, or by using a color-coding system for file subcategories. Whatever system you choose, the important thing is that all of your files are clearly labeled and in a location that makes sense, so you (and anyone else using your files) understand the filing system you implement. Keep your filing system straightforward, up-to-date, and intuitive for others. Remember, a good filing system can become your best defense against the paper problem, so keep up with it.

▣ ▣ ▣ ▣ ▣ Clutter Control Quickie: Post Things on a Bulletin Board

Consider hanging a bulletin board near your desk for those papers that demand top priority. Depending on the size of the bulletin board, you can divide it up into areas that are labeled, "To Do Today," "To Do Tomorrow," and "To Do Next Week," for example. Make sure you keep this board free of clutter by hanging only the most essential items. ▣

Just don't overfile, or you'll make your life harder. There's no point in making several trips to the filing cabinet throughout the day if you know you are definitely going to be using certain papers. Instead, group those things together logically. If you have a report to write, bundle all papers with relevant information into one group. Using a specific folder will help keep these papers together and in one place. Mark the folder clearly for quick access.

Paper Trays

Paper trays are great ammunition in the battle for office clutter control. They stack well, they don't take up a lot of room, and you can designate separate trays for specific purposes. Place papers you need to deal with right away in the top tray. Then, for papers you want to keep handy, but don't need at present, the second tray is a good option. You can also use a separate tray for items that need to be sent out, such as memos or letters, and another for items you need to file. Don't let these trays get too full! Keep them under control. Use them for easy access and practicality, not for procrastination and long-term storage.

Proper Mail Protocol

Maybe you handle your mail on a daily basis, or perhaps you prefer to leave it until the end of the week when you've sorted the rest of your paper. If you get a lot of mail at work, stacks upon stacks would probably accumulate on your desk if left for too long. But if things trickle in more slowly, it could be that all your incoming mail for the week might fit nicely into a mesh basket specifically for that purpose. Regardless of when and how often you choose to sort your mail, always do it next to a trash barrel. Don't even bother opening junk mail—it only wastes your time. For those pieces of mail you do open, immediately dispose of any advertisements or other unnecessary additions.

For Convenience Sake

Take a look around your office. Which items do you use the most? Are they within arm's reach, or do you have to cross the room to get to them? Even if things don't look cluttered, inconvenient placement can destroy an otherwise organized system.

Say, for instance, each day you repeatedly refer to a certain series of reference books located across the room. You know exactly where they are and are careful to keep them in order, but this is still a hindrance to your organizational system. You constantly have to stop what you are doing, get up, and walk across the room each time you need a book, so you break your concentration over and over. This gets bothersome, so you start to get lazy and don't return the books to their rightful places. Eventually, there's a heap of books on your desk, and then on the floor, since not all of them will even fit on your desk. Pages are getting torn and covers are getting bent. Now your office is a clutter-filled disaster area, and you can't find anything amid all those heavy books.

■ ■ ■ ■ ■ Clutter Control Quickie: Nix the Pics

Although it's tempting to surround your work space with lots of personal mementos and photos, resist this urge. Sure, having a few personal mementos, such as a picture of your kids, is important. But, too much of this stuff will only clutter up your desk space and create a distraction. Save the bulk of this stuff for the living areas of your home. ■

Surely, a little rearranging is in order. If you are panicking at the thought, don't. Yes, it might seem like a huge pain to rearrange your system, but there's probably an easy solution. Maybe there's a file cabinet or some other mobile object close to your desk that you can switch with the bookcase. Or, if switching one item with the other does no good because you need both things and can't cram them into one small space, then perhaps you don't need every single book near you, just those in the reference series. If so, you could put up a smaller hanging shelf next to your desk to keep those specific books within arm's reach. Get creative with your clutter-control solutions, and rearrange things for your own convenience.

Minor Details

If your office is anything like most, you have lots and lots of small stuff. There are probably a dozen items on your desk alone that regularly get misplaced or scattered. Pens, pencils, paper clips, staplers, rubber bands, thumbtacks, tape—do you ever waste time and energy looking for these items? If so, you need to apply the same rules that you did at home, and find the proper spot for everything you use at work. Small office supplies should be kept in a desk drawer that's readily available and within arm's reach, and they should not clutter your desktop when they aren't in use. Instead, purchase small containers to divide up your supply drawer so that it remains well organized and each item stored in that drawer is readily available. You can even use something as simple as cardboard dividers to keep the items from getting jumbled together. Just make sure you don't sabotage your own system by absent-mindedly throwing things in the wrong sections! On a regular basis, sort through the drawer and throw away dead pens, bent paper clips, stretched-out rubber bands, and other useless junk that gets accumulated.

Here are some other tips that will help you not to sweat the small stuff at the office:

• Invest in a desktop calendar that's large enough to pencil in appointments, notes, and any other information you need at a moment's glance. These also make it easier to check the progress of upcoming weeks, which will help you to keep your schedule uncluttered.

• Keep a small notebook by the phone, and mark the date on the top of a clean page each day. Use this page to make notes on telephone conversations you have, to remember details. If you sometimes need to take the information with you, use a carbon phone message pad, and tear off the top sheet so you won't have to recopy information.

• Store similar items together. For instance, you probably have a mélange of stationery products like letterhead, envelopes, and stamps, which can all be relocated to a more useful area, such as next to your Rolodex or beside the printer.

• Make a clean sweep at the end of each day: Settle everything into its proper home, replace anything you brought in from outside the office, and leave your work space looking as though it hasn't been touched.

• Don't forget to look over your to-do list and schedule for the following day. If you mark off tasks you've completed and make note of what you have left to do, you'll cut through your mental clutter and come in with a clearer head the next day.

Capitalizing on Your Computer

Whatever the location of your office, your computer is a fabulous resource when it comes to curbing clutter in your workspace. Think of the computer's hard drive (the place where your files, programs, and data are stored) as an electronic filing system to keep you organized. Eliminate unnecessary clutter from your computer so that you can find what you need as quickly and easily as you would if you were going through your paper files.

Simply by using your everyday programs, your computer generates random files that fill up your hard drive, even though you don't need them. For example, the Web browser Microsoft Explorer keeps track of every Web site you visit and stores detailed information about those sites in various cache and temporary folders and files. To delete some of the older Microsoft Explorer files you might not need, from the Tools pull-down menu in the program, select the Internet Options feature. You can then adjust the Temporary Internet Files settings or delete the unnecessary files.

▪ ▪ ▪ ▪ ▪ Clutter Control Quickie: Save Space with Your Monitor

If you're looking to save desk space, consider adding a flat-screen monitor to your computer. These monitors are often only several inches thick, yet they have excellent resolution. They're also easier on your eyes when using your computer for extended periods of time. Apple, CTX, Hitachi, Hewlett Packard, NEC, Mitsubishi, Nokia, Philips, Princeton Graphics, Samsung, Sony, and ViewSonic all offer flat-screen monitors in various sizes. ▪

If you're not confident about your computer savvy, try using a program like Norton SystemWorks *(www.symantec.com)* to help you manage your computer files and keep your system operating properly.

Backing Up Data

Periodically clean up your computer's hard drive and get rid of unnecessary files, data, and programs. Before deleting anything from your computer, however, make a backup of the files and data. Backup files can be stored on 3.5" disks, writable CD-ROMs, or ZIP disks, or by using some other form of data backup device. ZIP drives from Iomega *(www.iomega.com)* or any writable CD-ROM are easy to use and inexpensive.

You can also use a data-storage device, such as a ZIP drive, to scan paper-based files into your computer and store them electronically. Just make sure to save your work on a regular basis and then make daily or weekly backups of your most critical data. By converting some of your paper files in this way, you'll save a lot of clutter. Adobe Acrobat *(www.adobe.com)* is a great program to use for scanning and electronically storing paper-based files. You can convert files to Adobe Portable Document Format (PDF), which maintains the look and format of your original documents and can be opened reliably across a broad range of hardware and software.

▓ ▓ ▓ ▓ ▓ Clutter Control Quickie: Eliminate Electronic Clutter

Electronic clutter is often an insidious obstacle to organization. Think about it: At this moment, you probably have voice mail messages waiting to be played, e-mails loading up your in-box, and a hard drive you haven't cleaned out in ages. Clear as much as possible out of your "virtual" world on a daily basis. The more frequently you do this, the less likely it is to get out of control ▓

Organizing Your Home Office

Whether you work from home full-time or part-time, or you simply want to establish space in your home to handle your personal finances, taking the time to organize and unclutter your home office will boost your productivity and help you to feel in control of important business details. Before you can tailor an organizational system to suit your home office environment, create a detailed list of the types of work you'll be doing from this area of your home. Think about the tasks you perform, including brainstorming, making business phone calls, having teleconferences, meeting in person with clients or associates, paying bills, reading and doing research, or sending and receiving e-mail and faxes. Do you have office items that take up a lot of space and need to be properly stored, such as work-related and professional books, or a filing cabinet for business paperwork?

▓ ▓ ▓ ▓ Clutter Control Quickie: Storing Supplies

If you're working out of your home office, you probably don't have the benefit of a separate supply room. Things can get cluttered in a small office when you need to store paper, pens, files, notebooks, shipping supplies, and other essentials. These things need to be kept readily available, in a clutter-free manner. The best way to store these items is in a closet, in plastic storage bins or on extra shelving you add. ▓

Next consider what you might need to add or change in terms of furniture, office supplies, or equipment, to reduce clutter in your workspace. Make sure you have office furniture with plenty of drawers and file cabinets. Because your desk is the central and most integral part of your home office, decide on the best location for that piece of furniture first. Then determine what other furniture and equipment needs to be nearby and what can be placed elsewhere in the room. It will be easier to keep your home office from feeling cluttered if you position your desk properly and order basic work necessities in a more functional layout.

Creating the Right Work Environment

As mentioned in previous chapters, it's important, if possible, to maintain your office in an area that is closed off or at least separated from the rest of your living space. Unless you have an extra room in your home to spare for an office, however, this type of private space might be a tough commodity to come by. If space is an issue and right now you're feeling cramped and cluttered because your home office is squashed into a corner of the family room or bedroom, consider alternative spaces, such as your basement, garage, sunroom, guest bedroom, or even the attic, if you can finish it off in a way that's suitable for working.

Choosing the Right Desk

If you're having issues with clutter control in your home office, it probably has something to do with the shape, layout, or organization of your desk. You might already be using a rectangular-shaped desk, which is the shape that comes to most people's minds when they think about desks. When handling basic paperwork and other work necessities, however, this design is not always the most appropriate. The small central drawer and file-sized side drawers often don't provide enough storage space, and after you add a computer, printer, telephone, and a basic desk set to the top of a rectangular desk, most of the valuable work space is already used.

■ ■ ■ ■ ■ Clutter Control Quickie: Clear Your Desk

If clutter is crowding your desk, get serious about clearing your workspace. Instead of having file bins on your desk, take advantage of nearby wall space and set up hanging files. A computer monitor stand is another excellent way to save desk space. It also keeps your monitor at eye level, which creates a more comfortable work environment that inflicts less stress on your neck, shoulders, and arms. ■

Think about switching to a U-shaped or L-shaped design that provides ample desk space. For most people, desk space is a premium—you want to have as much open desk space as possible, based on the amount of room in your home office. If you're working with a tight squeeze, be sure to take good measurements so you can figure out how to fit the largest desk possible, yet not feel like this piece of furniture dominates the room or makes for a claustrophobic work space. Once your work space isn't so tight, it will be easier to stay on top of clutter control.

Keep important files, your computer (and printer), telephone, and/or other items within arm's reach to maximize productivity. To ensure that what you need is readily available, make a point of getting rid of nonessential furniture and other items that clutter up your home office space. For example, if you rarely use a calculator, keep it in a desk drawer, as opposed to on the desktop itself, or simply use the calculator built into Microsoft Windows.

Home Office Filing

Remember to keep your files, papers, and documents, whether they involve your professional work or personal business, in file cabinets or bins where they are readily accessible, yet out of the way when not needed. One of the most disorganized approaches you can take is allowing papers, receipts, and other documents to pile up on your desk, on the floor, or on chairs.

▪ ▪ ▪ ▪ ▪ Clutter Control Quickie: In and Out

Stave off clutter by using an in-box/out-box or a to-do box and place all of the papers you need to deal with, except for the ones you're currently working with, in there. This way, you'll know they're all stored in one place, so you can properly file them in a cabinet or throw them away once you have the time to sort through them. ▪

File cabinets come in a wide range of sizes, but in a home office space, it's an excellent strategy to use as much vertical space as possible by investing in a four-drawer file cabinet. Your most time-sensitive and important papers can be kept directly on your desk using stackable files—just make sure to be disciplined enough to process those important papers properly, so they don't sit there indefinitely.

Keep current files readily available, then figure out the best way to store older paperwork that you need to keep. You can invest in cheap manila envelopes or cardboard storage boxes (shaped like filing cabinets), or you can spend a bit more and purchase airtight plastic containers. Store this archived material in an out-of-the-way area, such as a basement or attic. If you really want to cut down on paper clutter in your home office, consider scanning old files into a computer and storing them on your hard drive, on a Zip Disk, or on a writable CD-ROM.

■ ■ ■ ■ ■ Clutter Control Quickie: Simplify Your Finances

If you feel like your finances are cluttered or out of control, you need to simplify. Go through a single bank for all your transactions. If you invest, go through a single firm. When possible, have your paycheck automatically deposited into your bank account and have payments debited automatically from your account or make them online so that you don't have to run to the bank or remember to mail things out all the time. ■

After you invest the initial time to unclutter your files, clean them out periodically to avoid clutter buildup. Spending fifteen minutes per day or an hour a week organizing your paperwork will save you countless time later and keep you more organized.

Planning to Be Productive

Whatever the location of your office, the best way to stay on top of clutter is to take an organized approach to your work habits. For example, after you create your to-do list each morning, allocate time to open your mail, deal with incoming e-mail, and do whatever other tasks are an important part of your routine. As you plan your day, expect to have some distractions, so don't overbook yourself. After all, emergencies happen, unexpected phone calls come in, and uninvited people drop by when least expected. Learning how to deal with unexpected situations will ensure that you remain focused on what you need to accomplish.

■ ■ ■ ■ ■ Clutter Control Quickie: Separate Business and Personal Paperwork

If you have a home office, intermingling your business and personal paperwork in the same filing cabinet is a recipe for organizational disaster. You don't want auto-related papers, banking, bills, letters from your kids' school, and so on to get mixed up with important financial, health/medical, insurance, investments, legal, or tax information for your business. Set up separate filing cabinets, then divide your files and label them carefully. ■

Implementing an organizational system can help you deal with everything from your papers to your professional responsibilities and give you parameters on what to keep, what to toss, and what to take action on.

Positioning your office space for success and good fortune isn't brain surgery, but it does require using your brain—and intuition. Be sure you've placed everything, from desk to file cabinets and bookshelves, in ways that serve you rather than detract from your goals. Once you've organized your office space, remember to stay on top of your clutter, because every piece of paper, outdated file, or inessential supply you keep without good reason will only add to the chaos in your work environment.

Work is a major part of your life, so be sure to deal with your work stressors. If you ignore them or let the negative effects pile up on you, eventually you're sure to reach a point where you're so overwhelmed you can't function any longer. Do what you can to avoid, eliminate, confront, manage, or balance chaos generated at the office, and you'll be on your way to living a more balanced, less stressful, and clutter-free life.

chapter 15

Lessening Your Laundry Room Mess

WHETHER YOU LIVE ALONE, have roommates, or are married with kids, no matter how often you do laundry, dirty clothing always seems to pile up. How often do you procrastinate this chore, to the point where you're rushing to wash a dozen loads because you're running out of essentials, only to end up with a drawer full of orphaned socks or a light-colored T-shirt stained with the dye from that new pair of jeans you forgot to wash separately? Everyone has had these laundry nightmares happen, but virtually all of these disasters can be avoided if you unclutter your laundry facilities and take a more organized approach to washing your clothes. By taking such steps, you can make doing laundry more bearable and reduce the chances of laundry mishaps.

Situating Your Laundry Area

One of the keys to having a well-organized laundry area is placement within your home. You might be lucky enough to have your washer and dryer situated in a convenient place, like off of your master bedroom or kitchen area, in a separate room. If you have your washer and dryer in the basement, however, there's a good chance that laundry piles up in other areas of your home, such as bathrooms or bedrooms, because you get sick of constantly lugging messy piles of clothing up and down stairs, so you avoid doing it unless it's actually time to throw a load into the wash. (If you're in this situation, consider installing a laundry chute.)

Having to carry countless loads of laundry up and down stairs will greatly increase the amount of physical exertion required for doing laundry. Likewise, the location of your laundry facilities will determine whether you can easily multitask (do your laundry while also handling other personal or household responsibilities). Unfortunately, however, washers and dryers are big and bulky, so finding a convenient place to install these appliances can be tricky. After all, you probably don't want to give up valuable closet space near your bedroom or in your master bathroom. Changing the location of your washer and dryer can also be a costly endeavor because plumbing, gas lines, and electrical wiring may have to be rerouted.

▪ ▪ ▪ ▪ ▪ Clutter Control Quickie: Stack Up

If your space is limited, consider purchasing a washer-dryer combo. These units can typically fit in a small closet. They do, however, have small load capacities. Washer-dryer combos come in two varieties: one that looks like a regular washer and dryer but stacks the dryer on top of the washer and one that is a single unit that both washes and dries clothes without you having to move the clothes from one unit to another. ▪

Don't fret if your washer and dryer aren't situated in the most convenient location—you can still cut your laundry clutter by better organizing this space in your home. In a perfectly uncluttered world, a laundry area would offer the following:

• Ample room for a full-sized washer and dryer (remember to leave at least a few inches between each of these appliances and the nearby walls)
• Shelving or cabinets to store detergents and fabric softeners (the room will look less cluttered if you use cabinets with doors so items can be stored out of sight)
• A space for keeping laundry baskets or hampers of dirty clothing
• An area for ironing, steaming, and folding clean clothes
• An area to hang wet clothing that needs to be line-dried
• Storage for hangers and/or a place to hang garments
• A sink for hand-washing garments

• A wastebasket

• Ample lighting, so you can clearly separate different-colored clothing, identify garments that are badly stained for special treatment, and read the handling instructions printed on the small labels of some garments

• Temperature control, because if the laundry area gets too cold (especially in a basement), the water pipes could freeze; if the room is too hot, it will be unbearable to actually work in the room

Thinking Strategically

This all sounds nice, but unless you live in a large house or have allocated a huge section of your basement to accommodate the above list of needs, chances are you'll have to improvise. Don't worry, it's possible to find easy solutions. Even taking the time to set up a simple clothing line outdoors will save you from cluttering up your basement with tons of clothes that need to be line dried—at least during the warm months of the year. If you don't have space in your laundry room to store hampers and laundry baskets of dirty clothing, quit using this as an excuse to throw all of your dirty clothes on the bathroom or bedroom floor and instead think strategically about how you can make room in your bedroom or bathroom closets to store these items until they are ready to be washed.

No matter where your laundry facilities are situated or how little space you have to work with, simply making sure everything you need is readily available and stored in the immediate area helps to reduce laundry clutter, so keep detergents and fabric softeners well organized and within close reach of the washer and dryer.

▦ ■ ■ ■ Clutter Control Quickie: Put Away Your Ironing Board

Never leave your ironing board in an upright position when not in use. This takes up too much space and adds a feeling of disorganization and clutter to any room.

Find an out-of-the-way place to keep your ironing board, such as in your linen closet or in the narrow space next to your washer or dryer, and *never* use the board as a spot for piling laundry—always fold and put away promptly. ▪

Nobody enjoys doing laundry, but everyone develops a personalized system for getting this tedious job done. The layout of your laundry facilities should not be haphazard or chaotic; it should complement your work habits in order to make this task as stress-free and easy as possible. If nothing else, try to carve out some space to separate your clothing into whites and colors when doing the laundry. This way, you'll be less tempted to leave your dirty clothes in a disorganized jumble all over the laundry room floor. You might also want to reserve some space to separate clothing based on which family member each garment belongs to or by fabric type. This space will also help you to avoid clutter when folding your clean clothes, because then you'll have some space to create piles, iron, and hang certain garments.

Following are some basic tips to simplify the process of doing your laundry, so that you're less apt to clutter this area of your home:

• Keep your dirty laundry sorted by color and fabric types so that it's easy to wash like garments together.

• Make a habit of emptying all pockets and then properly discarding or dispersing the various objects you find. Especially if you've got kids, it's easy to build an unwanted menagerie of tiny trinkets and toys that clutter your laundry room if you aren't careful.

• Turn down the cuffs of pants and shirts before they go into the wash—this will enable you to reduce wrinkles and also fold your laundry flatter, which saves space and hence reduces clutter.

• Deal with badly stained clothing separately, as soon as possible. Don't mix it in with the rest of your laundry; treat it with detergent or allow it to soak separately before putting it through a normal wash. This will save you the time and energy of sorting through a big mess to find the stained garment.

■ ■ ■ ■ ■ Clutter Control Quickie: Tips for Your Car

It's easy to control car clutter—just try a few of these ideas. Use a coin sorter to organize change for toll money and parking meters, and keep a sunglass holder, cellular phone holder/hands-free kit, and CD holder handy to store these key items efficiently. Also keep a plastic container in your trunk to store car-cleaning products. To keep your glove compartment organized, purchase a vinyl portfolio for storing maps and papers, like your registration and vehicle owner's manual. Then, once a month, sort through your glove compartment and throw away garbage and other useless items. ■

chapter 16

Targeting Other Trouble Spots

STORAGE SPACES LIKE THE BASEMENT, attic, and garage are often the most intimidating when it comes to attacking clutter. These are typically the very places that breed the most clutter because they serve as holding spots for all those large, cumbersome items and disparate odds and ends you just can't seem to find space for elsewhere. If you've been piling load after load of stuff into these spots for years and are now apprehensive about uncluttering it all, keep this in mind: An unorganized space holds far less stuff than a space that's properly ordered. Dive right in, get to work, and you'll soon see that you have more free storage space than you think.

Finding a Place for Everything

It is possible to turn your basement, attic, and garage into a useful storage facility—in fact, it can be done easily with the proper use of shelving, cabinets, hooks, and airtight storage bins. Select the best tools to beat clutter and the smartest spots to store your things appropriately. Remember, clutter control is all about making the fullest possible use of available space—not simply throwing items into it in an unorganized manner.

As you begin to reconfigure things in these parts of your home, stick to the following guidelines:

- Clean, package, and/or launder all things. Items that go into storage in good condition are more likely to stay that way longer. For example, polish your jewelry or silver flatware.

- Sort and place similar items together.
- Categorize.
- Place items in sturdy, airtight storage containers.
- Label each carton, container, or item with a proper description that's easily visible, such as "Summer Clothing," "Christmas Decorations," or "Winter Jackets."
- Store things in such a way that you can easily find and retrieve them without having to dig through endless piles of stuff.

Beating the Mess in Your Basement

Your basement can be an excellent storage location for a wide range of large and small items, such as extra furniture, sporting equipment, off-season clothing, and deck or patio accessories. If you're using your basement for storage, first examine the space carefully and determine potential hazards you'll want to take precautions against, like flooding, mold, mildew, rodents, insects, extreme temperatures, and so on. If, for example, the room is constantly damp, you might want to install a dehumidifier to help cut down or eliminate mold and mildew buildup. If flooding might become a problem, consider installing a sump pump. No matter what, make sure you have a smoke detector in your basement and check it at least every six months.

Don't just throw all of that residual clutter you've cleared out of your closets, bedrooms, family room, and other living areas down into the basement with no rhyme or reason. Take a few minutes to draw a rough layout of the area and determine how and where you'll be storing your various belongings, so that you can make the most efficient, logical use of your space.

▪ ▪ ▪ ▪ ▪ Clutter Control Quickie: Security Measures

If you live in an apartment or condo, access to extra basement or attic storage space can be a great bonus in the fight against clutter. Just be sure that if you share this space with other tenants or residents, you use containers that can be locked. Also use solid-colored storage containers (not clear or see-through), and don't visibly label the contents. Instead, number them and keep the list of the contents of each numbered container to yourself. ■

Don't carry anything down into your basement for storage until you've properly prepared the area. That means going through everything (yes, everything!) that's already stored there, emptying it out, and cleaning it thoroughly. Eliminate all unwanted clutter— throw away, donate, or sell anything that you no longer want or need or that is damaged beyond repair, and remove items that are blocking areas you want to use as work or play space.

Next, install shelving and other necessary organizational tools. (You can even use hooks and other hardware to help you create extra storage by hanging items from the basement ceiling.) You can visit a local hardware store to purchase shelving, or try some of these Internet-based companies:

• **Basis Design** *(www.basisdesign.com)* sells shelving and organization units that require no tools for assembly and are ideal for closets, cabinets, and other storage spaces.

• **1-800-BUY-RACK** *(www.buyrack.com)* offers industrial-strength shelving, racks, stacking bins, or other types of heavy-duty cabinets.

• **Dura** *(www.dura.co.uk)* sells modular metal storage units that combine cabinets, shelving, and pegboards. This storage system is perfect for your garage, basement, or workshop.

• **Shelving Direct** *(www.shelving-direct.com)* offers a line of boltless shelves, racks, bins, and workbenches that are appropriate for use at work and at home.

After the room is prepared, fill your basement with the items you plan to store there. Be sure to follow your diagram so that things get placed in the appropriate spots. Allocate space for larger items, such as furniture, bicycles, boxes, plastic storage containers, and luggage, first. After you decide what to do with the big stuff, focus on the smaller items you'll be keeping and what you need to store them properly. Devise the best combinations of boxes, shelving, cabinets, or even wall-mounted pegboards with hooks to help you cut clutter and make your basement space more usable.

As you evaluate your storage plan, answer the following questions:

• Are the items you're storing easy to find and readily accessible?
• Have you placed everything far enough away from your laundry area or workshop area? Is there a clear path to your working appliances, as well as ample space to work and play?
• If you have children, does your storage area provide any potential hazards? Should certain items be locked up separately?
• Have you protected your belongings against natural disasters (flooding, mildew, mold, insects, and rodents)?
• Are your stored items in the way of your home's hot water heater, furnace, fuse box, washer, dryer, or any other appliances in use within the basement? Are all drains and pipes clear from any obstruction?

If you're storing plastic crates or boxes, stack them up against a wall to ensure they are stable and won't fall. Also, make sure the labels describing what's in each box are facing outward and are easily readable. Place the larger and heavier boxes on the bottom and the lighter boxes above them. Items stored in boxes at the bottom of the piles should be the ones you'll be needing the least often, since it will take the most work to get to them.

Remember to divide and categorize what you'll be storing. Sports equipment should be kept together, as should books, furniture, holiday decorations (and gift wrapping supplies), and other similar items. Make sure you keep flammable items away from your furnace, hot water heater, washer, dryer, and any other potential dangers.

■ ■ ■ ■ ■ Clutter Control Quickie: Room to Move

If you also use your basement as a workshop, exercise room, hobby area, or play room, make sure you keep your storage area separate so you have enough room to do the things you want to comfortably. Use room dividers or any other methods that work for you to section off each area of your basement, as needed. ■

As you're placing various items, think in terms of when they'll be used, and try to group things together accordingly. For example, you might want to store your winter clothing in containers near your Christmas decorations. Likewise, you could store your grill near your Fourth of July decorations and lawn furniture. If you go on a family vacation every summer and use your luggage, keep it near your summer items for easy access.

Attacking the Junk in Your Attic

There's an age-old saying that goes, "Out of sight, out of mind." Just because you're able to hide your stuff in the attic and forget about it doesn't mean you should use this space for all of the clutter you move out of your primary living spaces. Hopefully, by this point, you've busted clutter from top to bottom in your home. Don't stop now—carry your efforts straight through to the attic-organization process.

Attics are typically more difficult to access than basements, so chances are, once items get thrown up there for storage, they're hardly ever seen and often tough to locate. Since attic space is often tight and tough to maneuver, it's best to reserve this space for storing lighter or smaller items, such as off-season clothing, empty luggage, holiday decorations, empty boxes from electronic equipment, toys, or sports equipment.

▓ ▓ ▓ ▓ ▓ Clutter Control Quickie: Tread Lightly

Don't place anything heavy on the floor of your attic unless you're confident the floor can bear the weight. If you need to store hefty items in your attic, you might want to reinforce the flooring by placing a thin wooden board across two or more support beams, and then storing some of your belongings on top of the board. ▓

If you need to unclutter your attic for extra storage, make sure you have easy access to the space. Consider replacing the basic access panel entrance (which you might need a ladder to get to) with a pull-down staircase. Also, install a light switch or light pull-string near the entrance to the attic. You won't ever be able to stay clutter-free in your attic if you can't even see what you're doing. For information on pull-down staircases, visit any hardware or home improvement store, or check out the Ladder Pros Web site *(www.ladderpros.com)*.

Organize your attic in much the same way you did your basement. In other words, keep in mind that you'll be storing your items in a non-climate-controlled environment that has potential hazards, and take the appropriate precautions. Unless you're using airtight containers, don't store paper-based items, such as photos, books, or other important documents, in the attic. Videotapes and audiocassettes as well as any type of electronic equipment won't do well in a potentially damp environment with extreme hot or cold temperatures.

▓ ▓ ▓ ▓ ▓ Clutter Control Quickie: Use Every Nook and Cranny

You can create additional storage space in your attic by maximizing the area behind attic knee walls. This wedge-shaped space is perfect for installing shelves, individual drawers, or rolling bins that you can pull out into the main area of your attic space when needed. ▓

As you did in the basement, consider what you plan to store in your attic, draw a rough layout of the area, and determine how and where you'll be storing your various belongings. Measure your attic space carefully, and figure out what you need to add to make it more usable. Clean your attic thoroughly, and be sure to get rid of all cobwebs. Sort through the items you're storing and place those that you won't need often in the back, where they're less readily available. As you rearrange things in your attic, make sure the air vents are unobstructed. Also keep items away from a ventilation fan if your attic has one.

Grappling with Garage Clutter

Negotiating the clutter control process in your garage can be a tall order. You most likely need this space for your car, yet you probably have a lawn mower, gardening items, bicycles, sports equipment, auto parts, and tools you need to store there as well. The garage is also a perfect spot to use for a workshop— assuming you have room for a worktable after you stuff all of those other things into this space!

Launch the same basic plan of organizational attack on your garage that you used on your attic and basement. As you are measuring, emptying your space, and assessing the storage solutions you need to add, make sure your car is parked inside the garage at first. Then take a piece of chalk and draw an outline of your car, so you know exactly how much space it will occupy. Include the space the car doors will take when opened, so you can get in and out of your vehicle comfortably. Then back your car out to make ample room for organizing!

■ ■ ■ ■ ■ Clutter Control Quickie: Room for Recyclables

If you store your recyclables in your garage, the best way to keep those items from cluttering up is using several large bins or garbage pails to separate aluminum cans, glass bottles and jars, and newspapers from your trash. Make sure the recycling bins you use for bottles and cans have tight lids so you can keep out wild animals. Ideally, bins with wheels are easiest to use. ▨

Clean your garage thoroughly. Then, place the items that need to be stored in the garage. Make sure all cartons, boxes, and crates are clearly labeled. If you have small children, remember to lock up all tools, chemicals, and other dangerous items. And be sure you install both a smoke detector and a carbon monoxide detector in your garage and check them every six months to ensure they remain operational.

The following sections share some organization tools and products designed specifically for a garage. Many of these items are available from hardware or home improvement stores, or they can be ordered directly from the Internet.

Garage Storage Cabinets

Garage Storage Cabinets *(www.gsc-cabinets.com)* offers a modular wall unit system that incorporates shelves, cabinets, and even a workbench. These mix-and-match cabinets are available in 12", 16", and 24" depths that are perfect for storing everything from gardening tools to automotive accessories. Designed to hang on a steel railing system, these fixtures get clutter off of your garage floor, prevent water damage, and allow you to reach beneath for easy cleaning. Because garage floors are poured at a sloping angle, the hanging system ensures that doors close smoothly, drawers slide easily, and cabinets hang straight for long-lasting performance.

Wood Logic Storage Products

Wood Logic Storage Products *(www.woodlogic.com)* is an online retailer of innovative products designed to organize a wide range of items typically stored in the garage. Check out the company's Woodpegger peg systems, vertical bike racks, and other hanging storage kits, to aid you in your quest for garage clutter control.

Stack-On Products Company

To keep track of and organize your tools, car parts, or other items, Stack-On *(www.stack-on.com)* offers a complete line of cabinets and garage-organization products. Stack-On Products Company is a leading manufacturer of top-quality tool storage systems, accessories, and security cabinets. Stack-On supplies a wide and diverse line of tool storage products to meet the needs of mechanics, maintenance personnel, tradespersons, home-owners, and hobbyists. Its product line includes steel and plastic hand boxes, specialty storage products, chests, cabinets, and steel security cabinets.

StoreWall

Instead of cabinets, StoreWall *(www.storewall.com)* offers a well-designed, contemporary variation of a pegboard with hooks for storing and displaying tools and other items. The Web site offers a wide range of accessories, including shelves, hooks, bins, baskets, and many specialty storage products to solve your toughest garage organization assignments. You can use StoreWall inside or outdoors (it's waterproof and can be easily cleaned), and the system is available in a variety of solid colors and wood grains. Each tongue-and-groove panel is ¾" thick, 15" high, and available in either 4' or 8' lengths.

Organize Everything

A stand-alone shelf unit is a quick, easy fix for the garage that requires no installation and sits freely on the floor. You can find lots of different options at any home-improvement or hardware store, or check out Organize Everything *(www.organizeevery thing.com)*. The InterMetro shelves are made of heavy-duty steel construction, can be adjusted up or down, and offer easy snap-together assembly. Each individual shelf holds 300 to 500 pounds.

Organize-It

Organize-It *(www.organizes-it.com)* offers a variety of different tools, hooks, and organizers designed for use in a garage. The Cord Wrap allows you to store extension cords neatly, while the Heavy Duty Lawn & Garden Rack keeps all of your gardening tools (large and small) in their proper place.

InterMetro

InterMetro's *(www.metro.com)* wire shelving will brighten any room of the house, but it's particularly useful in general storage areas like the garage. The company offers an extensive line of durable home shelving systems at a reasonable cost. The units come in a variety of colors and are easy to assemble. You can mix and match various pieces of this system to create customized shelving that suits your size specifications and needs. These products are available from hardware stores and authorized dealers nationwide.

▨ ▨ ▨ ▨ ▪ Clutter Control Quickie: Public Storage Facilities

If, after applying your best clutter-control efforts, the storage space available in your closets, basement, attic, and garage just isn't enough, consider using a public storage facility with a flat monthly or annual fee. Try Public Storage (800-44STORE, *www.publicstorage.com*) or Storage USA (800-STOR-USA, *www.sus.com*). To find other self-storage facilities in your area, go to Self Storage Net *(www.selfstorage.net)*, which offers a directory of facilities plus tips on how to maximize this type of storage space. ▨

chapter 17

Organizing the Outdoors

YOUR DECK OR PATIO might not be surrounded by four walls or bounded on the top and bottom with a floor and ceiling, but you can still make the most of your outdoor space in the same ways you would with any other room of your house. If you live in a warmer area, you can use your deck or patio practically year round, and in a more temperate location, you still have a good chunk of warm weather to enjoy relaxing, barbecuing, sunbathing, eating, and socializing outside. Don't waste this valuable spot. As with any living space, the trick to establishing organization outdoors is eliminating clutter in order to create a spot that is more functional and visually appealing.

If you want to curb clutter on your patio or deck, the first order of business is conserving space. Don't choose equipment and furniture that's too big for the area. Remember, you won't always be alone on your deck. If you throw a party or barbecue and have ten or more people using your deck space—not to mention the grill, table, and extra chairs—things can start to feel cluttered pretty quickly! Keep your patio or deck organized by storing unused items in a shed, garage, deck box, or some other unit away from the space you use, and don't leave lawn equipment and other items out in the open.

▪ ▪ ▪ ▪ ▪ Clutter Control Quickie: Use Your Railings

Make the most of the railings on your patio or deck—it's a great way to conserve valuable space and still decorate the area. Instead of placing flower pots on the ground, use flower boxes or over-the-rail planters. Many birdfeeders and other decorative items can be attached to the railing, and lighting can also be hung from walls or placed on railings to save even more space. ▪

Finding the Right Furniture

If you're considering adding some outdoor furniture to your deck or patio area or need to replace the furniture you already have because it simply feels too cluttered for your space, first consider the following:

• How much deck or patio space do you have available? Take careful measurements of your space, and also measure the furniture before purchasing it, to ensure all of the pieces will fit.

• Do you plan to eat outdoors? If so, consider a traditional table and chairs with enough room to accomodate several people and dishes comfortably.

• Will the furniture be kept on the deck year-round or stored during the off-season? If storage is necessary, do you have ample space in your garage, shed, or basement?

• What material would you like the furniture to be constructed from? Some materials hold up better than others outside, and the stronger and more durable the furniture, the easier it will be for you to keep things neat and clean.

• In addition to the patio furniture you choose, what else will be stored on the patio—a grill, plants, decorations, heating units, or fountains? The more things already taking up space on your deck or patio, the more careful you need to be when planning furniture placement.

Also make sure your patio furniture can be stored easily. If you plan to store it inside during the off-season, select models that will fit in your basement or garage without taking up too much space. Even if you choose pieces that can withstand various weather conditions, there will probably be times when you'll have to bring chairs and tables inside during extreme storms, so carve out a suitable space. (Whatever type of patio furniture you have, always store the cushions inside when they're not in use to avoid exposing them to the elements.)

If full-size patio furniture clutters your outdoor space, consider purchasing folding patio furniture. This way, you'll be able to bring out a table and chairs onto your deck or patio when dining or entertaining, yet replace these items with folding reclining chairs when you choose to relax and lie out in the sun. The Gardener's Supply Company (888-833-1412, *www.gardeners.com*) offers a line of extremely comfortable folding recliners that adjust to a variety of positions, yet fold up for easy storage in a shed, closet, garage, or basement.

The furniture you purchase should be sturdy and well manufactured, with firm seams and joints. Think about how much time you want to spend maintaining these things. Will the furniture require a lot of upkeep and maintenance, such as regular staining for wood or frequent cleaning? Be sure the patio furniture you choose can withstand all types of weather based on the climate you live in. It will be a lot easier to keep your deck or patio clean and organized if you choose low-maintenance pieces.

Now You're Cooking

The last thing you want in your outdoor space is a grill that is situated too closely to your deck or patio. Keep your grill several feet (or more) away from your sitting and eating area, and you'll not only help to control clutter, you'll be safer, too. If you only use your grill once every few weeks, during the spring and summer months, free up valuable space by storing it in a shed or garage (this is easy if you have a grill on wheels).

Keep all of your utensils near the grill. A small storage chest kept on your deck or patio is the perfect place for grilling utensils, citronella candles, and other useful items. Just don't store these things with other unrelated items, such as yard toys and sporting equipment. This will help to keep you organized, and if you have small children, it will ensure that they don't get hold of matches or other dangerous things.

Creating Outdoor Storage Solutions

You know you can't store all of your outdoor items on your patio or deck, and now you need to find a place for all of your garden hoses, sprinklers, shovels, and rakes when not in use. To avoid cluttering your basement, garage, or other in-house storage areas, you might want to organize an outdoor storage shed. These relatively small, stand-alone structures are built to withstand the elements and provide non-climate-controlled storage space outside the home.

Before settling on a solution for your outdoor storage needs, think about the following questions:

- What will you be storing in the shed?
- Will your storage shed be exposed to extreme weather conditions?
- Do the contents in your shed need to be kept waterproof?
- Does the shed have to be temperature-controlled?
- Will you need electricity in the shed?
- Where on your property will the shed be built or situated?
- Based on what will be stored, what size shed do you need? For example, if you have three bicycles, a lawnmower, and a leaf blower, these items will take up a lot more space than if you just have some gardening tools and toys.

Plastic storage sheds are available in a variety of shapes, sizes, and orientations: horizontal or vertical, top- or front-loading, with lifting or sliding roofs. Many require only simple assembly, so there are no long hours of building involved, and they usually need little or no maintenance. In addition to being

easy to construct and designed to fit visually into any landscaped environment, most storage sheds are durable. Sheds
with tough resin construction provide great protection for the
items inside.

▨ ▨ ▨ ▨ ▨ Clutter Control Quickie: Instant Shed

If you're looking for a fast solution for your outdoor clutter, Rubbermaid
(*www.rubbermaid.com*) offers several relatively inexpensive, freestanding,
weather-resistant storage sheds made from interlocking panels that assemble
in less than thirty minutes. Priced from $200 to $400, models such as the Large
Horizontal Storage Shed, Large Vertical Storage Shed, and Sliding-Lid Storage
Shed offer anywhere from 32 to 92 cubic feet of storage space. These units can
contain three separate shelves and can be anchored into the ground or attached
to the house. ▨

If, however, when you think of a backyard shed, a heavy-
duty plastic storage unit is not exactly what you have in mind,
you can easily find other types of small, stand-alone structures
in a range of styles and colors. There are plenty of sheds made
from other materials such as wood or metal that resemble
small barns or even tiny houses. These types of sheds can often
be custom-built to meet specific size requirements. Try
Backyard America, a company that sells a wide range of outdoor storage solutions via the Internet (703-392-5152,
www.backyardamerica.com), for a variety of storage sheds, some
of which even include vinyl siding, windows, shutters, and
doors. The Mini Barn, a traditional barn style, is useful and
compact, measuring 4' x 8' x 8'. The company offers a variety
of other utility and lean-to sheds, from 2' x 4' x 4' to sizes as
large as 10' x 8' x 8'.

▨ ▨ ▨ ▨ ▨ Clutter Control Quickie: Fetch a Hideaway Bench

Patio storage benches are another efficient method for outdoor clutter control—you can store your stuff and still have a place for your guests to sit.

Rubbermaid's model comfortably seats two adults, fits well just about any-where, and measures 48" x 25" x 36", with 4 cubic feet of storage space. It's perfect for storing gardening tools, hoses, cushions, and other small items. The Step2 Company (800-347-8372, *www.step2company.com*) also offers the Wicker Weave storage bench or seat, which features a weather resistant storage compartment for cushions, grill accessories, and other tools. ▦

Backyard America also offers an exclusive, under-deck shed system. These custom-built outdoor storage solutions are available in a variety of exterior finishes, door and window styles, and flooring choices. In addition to storage, these struc-tures can be used for potting, as playhouses, and as pool/spa cabanas.

There are also plenty of gardening-supply stores and nurs-eries that sell various types of sheds and outdoor storage solu-tions, so go and check some of them out.

Organizing Your Space

In addition to your lawnmower, leaf blower, gardening equip-ment, bicycles, and other large items, your shed is an ideal place for storing smaller items. Place these smaller items on shelves or in a special area where they're easily reachable without having to remove larger items. Also, keep the items you'll be using the most often closest to the front door of the shed for easy access. Items you'll use less frequently should be at the back corner of the shed, where they're not as readily accessible. Remember, the more you need to move stuff around, the more chance you have of clut-tering up your space.

Make sure to install plenty of hooks and shelves in your out-door storage area—it's an excellent use of space. You can use hooks to hang certain types of tools and other items. This will keep them out of the way, yet easily visible so you can retrieve them whenever they're needed.

One word of caution: Even if you have extra storage space, it doesn't mean you should allow your shed to become an alternate clutter storage location. Just as you've learned to do within your home, discard unwanted or unneeded clutter—don't let those broken tools and unwanted flower-pots pile up!

Controlling Tool Clutter

Now that you have this great shed, there's no need to throw all of your outdoor tools in it and then shut the door without a second thought. Do a little research, and you'll find a tool organizer that's just right for your space. Try some of these options, and your shed is sure to be clutter-free in no time.

For hanging tools with long handles, like rakes and shovels, the Long Handle Tool Organizer is perfect for your garage or utility closet wall. This 19"-long wall bar attaches with supplied screws, and three grippers support round handles from ¾" to 1¼" in diameter. This bar can even hold very heavy weights like sledgehammers. You can check this particular model out in the Garrett Wade Tool Catalog (800-221-2942, *www.garrettwade.com*), but similar products are available at most hardware stores.

The SureLock from Tidy Garage (888-4-GARAGE, *www.tidygarage.com*) is another wall unit that allows you to organize shovels, brooms, rakes, and various hard-to-store items in one compact place. The SureLock Tool Organizer mounts easily to any wall; its two self-adjusting, spring-locking arms hold any handle size and shape tool securely with the heavy, sharp parts nearest to the ground. Six large, permanently attached hooks offer a multitude of valuable storage options.

The Garden Rover, available from Plow & Hearth (800-494-7544, *www.plowhearth.com*) is a compact, mobile unit on wheels that's ideal for storing large and small garden tools. Load it with up to eighteen tools and push it to your work site. The four-compartment front pouch holds hand tools, seed packets, and other garden supplies and is made of vinyl-backed 600-denier fabric. It's lightweight and well constructed, and it has a 100-pound capacity to hold bags of mulch or seed. The 8" molded tires are designed so that the unit can be pulled or pushed along rough terrain.

The Plant Factory (334-653-7043, *www.net5.com/~plant factory)* offers the Fiskars Bucket Tool Caddy Plus, which turns any five-gallon bucket into the ultimate tool organizer for your garden. It has nineteen exterior and eleven interior pockets, guaranteed to keep all of your gardening tools and accessories uncluttered.

The Harriet Carter Garden Tool Organizer (800-377-7878, *www.hcgifts.com*) is a metal, floor storage caddy that allows you to keep your rakes, brooms, shovels, and other tools standing upright in storage. The caddy's twenty slots store tools neatly in place, plus there's a side rack to hold a garden hose. There's even room for pots, fertilizer, trowels, seeds, and more. The unit fits easily in a garage, greenhouse, basement, or utility closet.

Become an Über-Organizer

If you have the ambition to organize every single aspect of your gardening and landscaping, you might consider using a PC-based software package called Garden Organizer Deluxe (from PrimaSoft). For example, the Plant Organizer allows you to catalog your favorite plants (enter plant name, description, attributes, maintenance notes, pictures, and more). Other functions built into the software include an idea organizer to store information about different garden solutions, a work organizer to organize new garden projects and maintenance tasks, an address organizer to organize your garden-related contacts, and a Web resource organizer to keep track of Web links related to gardening and landscaping. Before you purchase a full version of the software, you can download a free, fully functional trial version from PrimaSoft's Web site, *www.primasoft.com.*

chapter 18

Staying Clutter-Free

NOW THAT YOU'VE SYSTEMATICALLY CUT through clutter in every room of your home—and hopefully learned to keep your stress levels in check and time management skills sharp in the process—all that's left is learning how to maintain your organizational efforts. This is a tall order, but think of the alternative—ending up right back where you started, drowning in a sea of clutter. The sections in this chapter remind you of some of the key tips you've learned and provide suggestions for staying a step ahead of clutter to help you to remain organized.

Keeping Up with Clutter

Even if you've rearranged your house top to bottom, organized your office, and uncluttered your outdoor space, your job is in no way done. Clutter control is an ongoing effort. Following is a recap of key strategies that will help to keep your momentum going so that you can keep up with clutter control.

Implementing Regular Clean-outs

The chapters in this book show you how to identify and deal with clutter in various areas of your home. But clearing out clutter is not a one-time-only task. To continue your organizational efforts, you must dig through all areas of your home periodically and distinguish between the belongings you need or want and the items that can be thrown away, donated, filed, or put into storage. Remember, if an item hasn't been used in several months or years and has no importance or sentimental value, it's time to chuck it!

Changing Your Behavior

You can eliminate every inch of clutter in your home, but until you get to the root of what's causing it, you'll never succeed in ridding yourself of the mess for good. For example, think about the different routines you automatically perform every day, and see if you absentmindedly breed clutter at certain times or in particular places. When you get undressed at night, for instance, do you throw your dirty clothes on the floor, where they all eventually pile up in a messy heap? If so, make it a habit to place the clothes directly in a laundry hamper instead. Remember, clutter comes in many different forms. Once you've pinpointed your sore spots for clutter, address the underlying issues.

Finding the Proper Place

After you decide on the appropriate spot for keeping all of the items in your home, you'll have little trouble finding things. What might give you trouble, however, is constantly remembering to put a tool, piece of paper, or any other object back in its proper place as soon as you're done using it. Try to be consistent with putting things away, and resist the urge to leave it till later. Adopting this practice not only helps you stay organized, it also greatly reduces the amount of time you will spend cleaning your home in the future, because it's easier to keep up with things a little bit at a time.

Grouping Similar Items Together

When organizing a closet, bin, cabinet, dresser drawer, medicine cabinet, or any other type of storage unit, remember the first step is emptying out all the contents of what you're organizing. Eliminate clutter and rid yourself of anything that's no longer wanted or needed. Then group similar items together. Finally, put your items back in an organized manner, giving each item or group of items a proper place.

Taking Advantage of Organizational Tools and Gadgets

If you look through mail-order catalogs, you'll find an abundance of organizational tools and useful gadgets on the market. Be sure to use plenty of these accessories, such as drawer dividers, specialty hangers, baskets, shoe racks, belt racks, jewelry organizers, and extra closet rods to maximize storage space and keep items well ordered and separated from each other.

Making the Most of Every Possible Storage Space

If you're tight on storage space, think of inventive ways to use unexpected areas. Install shelving above doorways and near the ceilings of a room, and add hooks, racks, or compartments to the back of doorways (inside closets, for example). Areas such as your attic, garage, and basement also offer additional storage opportunities.

Using Technology to Stay Organized

A personal digital assistant (PDA), such as those from Palm and Handspring, are ideal tools for keeping your schedule clutter-free. These versatile handheld units can also store thousands of addresses and phone numbers and complete a wide range of other tasks. If you tend to write messages for yourself on many different pieces of scrap paper that end up stuffed in your pockets or strewn all over your home, a PDA will help you to nip your disorganization in the bud by storing all of your information in one place for easy reference.

Creating Detailed To-Do Lists

Save yourself some serious mental clutter and be sure to write all of the things you need to do—personal, work-related, and social objectives—on one list every day. This list should include day-to-day tasks, such as errands, meetings, appointments, phone calls to make, and e-mails to write. It should also include tasks that bring you closer to achieving long-term personal, professional, and financial goals. After you create your to-do list, prioritize each task and input the appropriate information into your personal planner, PDA, or other scheduling tool. Ideally, you want to plan for as many things as you think you can accomplish in the course of your day, while still leaving time to deal with unexpected events.

Your to-do list is also a great place to keep track of things you need to do around the house to keep it uncluttered, organized, and clean. When you're about to embark on a massive cleanup or reorganization project, writing a to-do list helps you clearly define your objectives, create a time frame, and take a well-thought-out approach to your efforts.

For the day-to-day tasks that are necessary to run your home and keep it clean, follow these basic steps:

1. Create a list of what tasks you need to do (for example, cleaning the bathroom, doing laundry, changing bed linens, vacuuming, washing the kitchen floor, going to the dry cleaner, mowing the lawn, and so on).
2. Determine how often each of these tasks needs to be done.
3. Use a calendar, PDA, scheduler, or personal planner to construct a schedule for accomplishing these tasks, one at a time. For example, cleaning the bathroom may take thirty minutes after work on Mondays. Trips to the dry cleaner can be done on Tuesdays and Thursdays on the way to work or when dropping your kids off at soccer practice.

Clearly delineated project lists will help you to feel less overwhelmed by the prospect of encroaching clutter. After you create a to-do list for keeping your home clean and organized, stick to it so that it becomes part of your ongoing routine.

Working Toward Achieving Your Goals

After you set long-term goals for yourself, determine exactly what it will take to achieve your projects. Divide up each long-term goal into a series of short-term or medium-term goals that are more easily achievable. After you create a series of smaller goals, develop a time frame and set specific deadlines for reaching those goals. Each time you accomplish one of these smaller goals, you'll be that much closer to achieving one of your long-term goals, and that will motivate and encourage you along the path toward maintaining solid clutter control.

Cleaning the House

It's easy to revert to familiar patterns that allow clutter and disorganization to slip back into your life, especially at home, where things can get crazy if you're juggling a family and lots of other responsibilities. Don't sit back and wait until things start to fall apart again—be proactive! The best way to keep things under control is to come up with a basic housecleaning routine you know you'll stick with.

Most likely you've never put a lot of conscious thought into setting up a cleaning schedule for yourself. This might sound a little strange at first, but think about all of the chores you need to fit in to keep a clean, clutter-free house: There's dusting, scrubbing, mopping, vacuuming, glass and window washing, picking up, and airing out to be done. Sure, this sounds rough, but don't sweat it. We're not talking about the kind of schedule that keeps you cleaning nonstop. Not all of this needs to be done at once, *every* time you clean the house. Stagger your chores in a way that works for you.

Biannual Cleaning

You can probably handle doing a quick pickup here and there every day or dusting and vacuuming once a week, but let's face it—you just don't have the time to clear out your attic during the course of a regular week. If you want to give yourself a periodic clutter-control boost, plan two heavy-duty cleanings a year. It's ideal if you spread them out, with six months between each. These sessions are going to be pretty arduous, so be sure to schedule them for points in the year when you know you'll have some downtime.

Depending on the size of your home, it could take you a few hours or a few weeks. These cleanings are the time to sort through all of the new junk you've inadvertently acquired during the course of the past six months. Every single item in your home should be touched during this cleaning spree. Remember, if you don't do a thorough job with this now, you will have to spend even more time on it later. These two cleanings will serve as the foundation for the upkeep of your home. If you get your house super-clean now, it will be much easier—and more pleasant—to maintain your clutter control later.

▩ ▩ ▩ ▩ ▩ Clutter Control Quickie: Keep a Fix-It List

Biannual cleanings are a good time to take stock of maintenance issues in your home. While you're working, keep notes on what needs to be done. If there is a hole in a closet wall or your roof leaks a little, write it down. Once you're done cleaning, try to plan a schedule to have these things fixed within the next six months (if finances allow) so problems won't carry over from one cleaning to the next. ▩

Keeping up with clutter control at home need not be a major effort. Here are some other quick tips for keeping your house shipshape that will save you a lot of time:

• **Dusting can make all the difference** when it comes to a seemingly spotless house versus a dirty one. Dusty surfaces are the first things that people notice, so if you don't have the time to clean your house, but you are expecting company, give things a quick dusting.

- **Use a spray cleaner** to dust every two weeks or once a month, depending on your time schedule. This will help the condition of your furniture and give the house a deeper cleaning.
- **Always dust before vacuuming.** If you are going to give the entire house a once-over, work your way from the top down. You'll save yourself a lot of time—and you'll keep your house cleaner—if you stir the dust up and then suck it right into the vacuum.
- **Don't waste a lot of time on scrubbing.** There are several products on the market that keep scrubbing to a minimum, including shower cleaners you can spray after each use to cut down on soap and mildew buildup; toilet bowl disks that emit a cleaning solution every time you flush; and spray cleaners that break down grease buildup on their own, so you only have to wipe things down.
- **Put things away after each use.** This might sound simple, but it makes a big difference. Think about how it feels to walk into a house where items are haphazardly slung everywhere. You get the feeling that the house desperately needs a good cleaning, even if it's not dirty at all. Never underestimate the power of perception.
- **Designate certain days for doing particular chores.** For example, make Monday bathroom cleaning day, and make Thursday dusting and vacuuming day. This way, you'll fall into the habit of getting things done and out of the way. Or, if you prefer to clean room by room, schedule the living room one day and the kitchen the next.
- **Make use of your delegation skills.** If you're not the only one who lives in the house, you shouldn't be the only one responsible for keeping it clean!

Remember, your home is Grand Central Station for the rest of your life. It's your primary point of departure and arrival each day, and the central place for many important activities in your life. Stay as organized as you can at home, because the condition and organization of your home sets the tone for everything else you do. If things run smoothly at home, chances are things will also run smoothly in other areas of your life. By keeping your home life clutter-free, you'll be able to start and end each day on a peaceful note, which will keep you feeling focused, energized, and on the right track.